Oriental Rugs
from A to Z

J. R. Azizollahoff

Schiffer
Publishing Ltd

4880 Lower Valley Road, Atglen, PA 19310 USA

Dedication

"In memory of my mother, Pearl Azizollahoff"

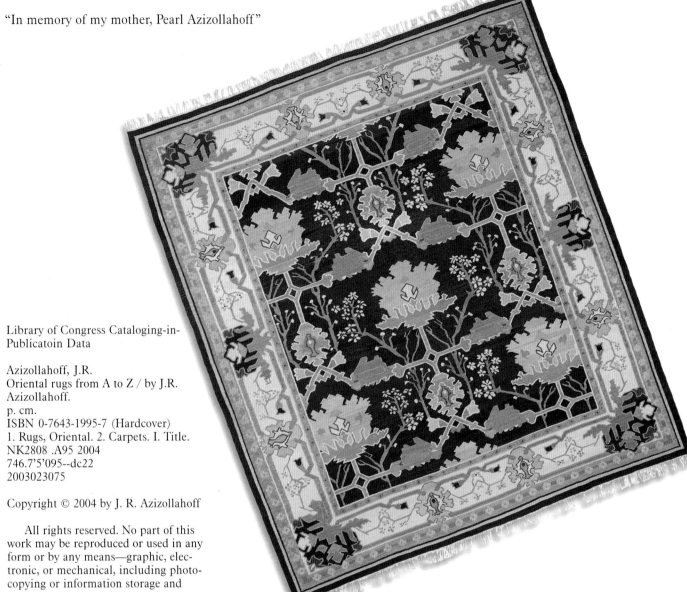

Library of Congress Cataloging-in-Publicatoin Data

Azizollahoff, J.R.
Oriental rugs from A to Z / by J.R. Azizollahoff.
p. cm.
ISBN 0-7643-1995-7 (Hardcover)
1. Rugs, Oriental. 2. Carpets. I. Title.
NK2808 .A95 2004
746.7'5'095--dc22
2003023075

Designed by Bonnie M. Hensley
Cover design by Bruce Waters
Type set in AdineKirnberg /Aldine 721 Lt BT

ISBN: 0-7643-1995-7
Printed in China
1 2 3 4

Published by Schiffer Publishing Ltd.
4880 Lower Valley Road
Atglen, PA 19310
Phone: (610) 593-1777;
Fax: (610) 593-2002
E-mail: Info@schifferbooks.com

For the largest selection of fine reference books on this and related subjects, please visit our web site at
www.schifferbooks.com
We are always looking for people to write books on new and related subjects. If you have an idea for a book please contact us at the above address.

This book may be purchased from the publisher. Include $3.95 for shipping. Please try your bookstore first. You may write for a free catalog.

In Europe, Schiffer books are distributed by
Bushwood Books
6 Marksbury Ave.
Kew Gardens
Surrey TW9 4JF England
Phone: 44 (0) 20 8392-8585;
Fax: 44 (0) 20 8392-9876
E-mail: info@bushwoodbooks.co.uk
Free postage in the U.K., Europe; air mail at cost.

Contents

About the Values ————————————————

The prices of carpets illustrated herein are approximate retail values as of August 2003 and are the opinion of the author. The prices may or may not correspond to the prices that ABC Carpet & Home charges for these rugs. Neither the publisher nor the author assumes any liability for variances in the pricing of any of the carpets illustrated herein. Numerous carpets illustrated herein are trade-marked and or copyrighted by their creators or owners and may not be reproduced without the express written consent of the publisher or author.

The Only Good Rug is the One You Love.

Acknowledgments

I wish to thank Jerome Weinrib, Chairman of the Board of ABC Carpet & Home, for permission to reproduce the close-ups and full-sized pictures from his inventory of rugs. Also, I would like to express my gratitude to Graham Head, President of ABC Carpet & Home, for his trust and support.

In addition, I am indebted to Alex Kimia, Senior Executive Vice President, and Manter Ho, buyer of fine Oriental rugs, at ABC Carpet & Home for their generous assistance with the transparencies.

I would like to express my appreciation to Leslie Stroh, publisher of *Rug News* in New York, for permission to reproduce some of the ideas I developed as an editor at the magazine between December 2000 and August 2003.

In addition, I am indebted to my editor, Jeffrey Snyder, and publishers, Peter and Nancy Schiffer, at Schiffer Publishing for all their help with this venture.

Finally, I would like to thank my wife, Li Kwang, for her love, support, and patience throughout this endeavor, as well as her advice about the organization of the transparencies.

Introduction

The purpose of this book is to help laypersons to understand new Oriental rugs. These ideas were developed over many years of buying, selling, and researching the subject of Oriental carpets. It is hoped that an educated consumer will buy more rugs either as floor coverings or for their possible collectible value.

In this era of Oriental carpet commercialization, both the rug novice and connoisseur must try to find the most distinctive and best quality rugs at the best possible price. This is the only way that Oriental rugs can and will remain items of great value·in the West.

Because of the mass marketing of Oriental carpets, more people have access to magnificent and long-lasting examples of art underfoot than any time in the past. The position taken here is that the tradition of Oriental rugs as objects of real value continues until this day, and will continue in the future, for the educated and discriminating buyer. The goal of the book is to help maintain or restore, in some small way, the glory and majesty of the Oriental carpet.

Because of the lack of significant public interest in semi-antique rugs, about fifty years old, and the scarcity of antique rugs, about eighty years old, new rugs only are featured and accompany relevant sections of the book.

Close-up photographs of carpets were taken by the author to exemplify certain principles and stimulate an appreciation of the areas of local interest in a particular rug which are often neglected by the private retail buyer. The power and majesty of the Oriental carpet cannot be fully appreciated unless viewed from up close and from a distance.

Unless otherwise indicated, all rugs and flatweaves illustrated are wool with cotton foundation threads.

All rugs illustrated are courtesy of ABC Carpet & Home in New York City and Hackensack, New Jersey.

Chapter One
Rug Quality

High Definition

High design definition is the most important element in carpet quality. A rug with a lower number of knots per square inch may have higher definition than a rug with a higher number of knots per square inch. Generally, the finer the carpet, the shorter the pile in order to enhance definition, whereas the coarser the rug, the longer the pile and the lower the definition.

High design definition is not as essential to new "antique washed" rugs whose designs are less crisp than slightly washed rugs. Nonetheless, chemically washed rugs should still have fairly crisp designs if they have been successfully washed. High internal contrast beneath the antique patina must be maintained in the new reproduction just as it is found in the old prototype. Study the old classic carpets in museums, old rug books, and old Sotheby's and Christie's catalogues to see the standard of high definition against which the new reproductions may be measured.

High definition in carpet design is similar to the greater sharpness and precision that is found in high definition color television. Sharp and powerful designs often have a sculpted three-dimensional quality as they float upon majestic background colors.

Chinese silk, close-up of center medallion. Chrome dyes, fine weave, very high definition.

Chinese silk, close-up, chrome dyes. Crisp, powerful design, beautiful top colors.

The state of the art in new Oriental rugs is the finish or wash. The chemical wash today is better and less harmful to wool and dyes than in the past. The soft lime and herbal wash at the end of the rug finishing process has very little negative effect upon the integrity of the carpet and reputable carpet retailers only buy from manufacturers who do not employ harsh and caustic chemicals in the antique wash. Good retailers know that carpets that have a heavy chemical wash will not retain the beautiful luster when commercially cleaned at a later time. Also, some manufacturers achieve the antique look by using pale colored wool that is not washed with chemicals at all.

Producers and importers take more pride in the finish or patina of their rugs than any other aspect of carpet production. The idea is to get a new rug to look exactly like a sixty to eighty year old carpet. Manufacturers cannot perfectly replicate the patina of the antique carpet because of the differential rates of color loss and oxidization in old rugs but they are getting very close to the exact look of the prototypes.

Pale and soft colored carpets are the perfect foil for the busy and colorful fabrics that most people purchase at the beginning of room decoration. The reason they are so popular is because they blend so well and easily with the deeper and more saturated colors of the adjacent fabric. They represent the solution to the omnipresent problem of busy wall, drapery, and chair fabrics.

Some experts believe the beauty of the old rug is in the patina which gradually develops over time through wear, exposure to light, and successive commercial washings. The colors then meld together in a pale or pastel totality that is integrated and harmonious. In order to get the best of both worlds, buyers should look for a finely woven, vegetal-dyed, antique-washed rug with good design definition that provides the beauty and opulence of fine detail and the softness and harmony of an antique rug. The best antique-washed carpets usually have at least one breathtaking color to stimulate the heart and enough local interest to arouse the mind.

A slight drawback to chemical washing is that it dries out the wool and cotton foundation of the rug. This results in a small and often insignificant loss of durability in the chemically washed carpet that is compensated for by the great beauty of many of these rugs. The design definition must however be fully maintained and not washed away by the chemical wash. The light antique wash will both maintain design definition and protein or oil levels in the cotton foundation and the wool pile on the surface of the carpet.

Many rug experts have been critical of antique washing in the past; however, this is a new revolutionary era of the "gentle Oriental" and the old purist critiques of heavy chemical washing no longer apply. The antique wash is no longer a trick foisted upon an unwary public by an itinerant salesman who claims that the rug is antique; rather, it is only through the light chemical wash that the carpet could meld with the busy adjacent fabrics so common to the large American home.

Soft and pale rugs lighten a room which contains dark fabrics or is not exposed to much sunlight. They are easy to match with adjacent fabrics because they often contain only a few soft colors that are so harmonious that they form a unitary overall value or tone. If one has a tight budget, one can save money by being one's own decorator. This is one of the reasons for the great popularity of these carpets.

Pakistan, close-up, vegetal dyes. Soft, unifying patina.

Pakistan, close-up, vegetal dyes. Harmony of the "gentle Oriental."

Chinese soumak flatweave, close-up, chrome dyes.

It is easier to understand rugs now than at any other point in the history of Oriental rugs in the United States because pedigree in carpets no longer exists today. In years past, the pedigree of Persian, Caucasian, Turkoman, or Turkish rugs guaranteed their value in the old rug trade. Today, the state of the art in rug production is in India, Pakistan, and China, which are countries rather than localities so that no local village or town pedigree is present.

Pedigree today is found in the specific style of high quality carpets from particular workshops which are discernible and inimitable. In the future, design and color rather than the knot shape of earlier rugs with village or town pedigree will probably distinguish these rugs.

If the carpet budget is sufficiently high, ask the salesperson to find the best workshop rugs from the East and compare them to one another. There are several rug producers today who are making carpets with all the characteristics of the great old weavings of the past that should be sold and resold in the old carpet market in the future if kept in good condition. The Eastern producer probably deserves most of the production credit as he keeps the important craft secrets even from the largest Western importers.

Good workshop rugs are always perfectly and symmetrically woven without the slightest imperfection in weave. In the best workshops today, weaving error never compromises the natural order or perfection of the Oriental carpet. Americans should not tolerate imperfections in design symmetry or quality control just as flaws are always rejected in the East.

The better the workshop, the more forgiving future old rug dealers may be about their condition. Distinctive rugs of average quality will have to be kept in perfect condition to be of value in the future, but a small degree of lowering of pile may be acceptable in a few rugs produced by the very best workshops today.

A price of about $50 a square foot at retail may be enough to pay for the carpet with workshop pedigree, but $60 a square foot and up obtain safer buys for the long term investment.

Pakistan, close-up, vegetal dyes. Inimitable workshop product.

Oppsosite page:

Top: India, close-up, vegetal dyes. Highly consistent contemporary classic.
Bottom: India, close-up, vegetal dyes. Popular and distinctive.

Twist and Ply

Rug quality is difficult to judge based upon the twist and ply of the wool or cotton because neither the public nor the rug salesperson can untwist the fibers to analyze them. Generally double-plied (pile) and double-weft rugs (two weft threads between each row of knots) are preferred because they have a higher specific gravity, weight, or density of pile than single plied and single weft carpets; however, there are exceptions to this rule in the sense that better wool may be found in a single plied, single weft than a double-plied, double-weft carpet. Thus a single ply, single weft rug with better wool may be more durable that a double ply, double-weft carpet with inferior wool.

In addition, the nature of the generally cotton foundation is significant in that some rugs may have thin, single plied cotton warps and wefts which yield a carpet with a low specific gravity or lighter weight. Such a rug may not be as durable as a rug with thicker, double-plied cotton warps and wefts. The warp and weft threads should be tightly twisted when single plied and tightly twisted together when double-plied. The pile may be more loosely spun and plied.

The great old Persian rugs, such as the Sarouk and Heriz, had heavily bodied, tightly spun cotton foundations that could not wear out even when all of the wool pile was worn away. The Persian Bidjar had an indestructible, tightly packed hard back or foundation in well-twisted wool or cotton. The reason why many old Persian carpets may be extensively refurbished and tinted is because the quality of the generally thick cotton warp and weft threads was excellent.

A spectacular rug with a low specific gravity and loosely spun fibers may break all rules and still be an excellent, albeit delicate, carpet.

India, close-up, chrome dyes. Fairly high fiber density or specific gravity.

Iranian flatweave, close-up, vegetal dyes. Tightly spun and plied wool.

Durability

Durability is difficult to measure by sight or touch but it is possible to get an idea of how long a rug may last through the senses. The great old Persian rugs of the past had life spans of approximately 150 years because the pile and foundation threads had a high specific gravity or density and high tensile strength. Since they were only soap washed when new, the oils that stuck the knots together and kept all the fibers elastic over time remained intact. The rugs thus remained strong and their knots tightly twisted together. The drying out of fibers over time makes rugs more susceptible to wear.

The more thick strands of cotton that are tightly plied together, the thicker and stronger the foundation. The thinner cotton weft threads running across the loom horizontally should also be tightly plied together to form a solid foundation.

A rug may have heavy, dense pile and a densely packed cotton foundation and may have great durability. Or a rug may have a less dense pile and a very hard, tightly twisted foundation. Such a rug may have a slightly shorter life span.

Generally, thick piled rugs with thick foundations are preferred in rugs with lower knots per square inch at the low and middle price points. The pile should also be fairly long to maintain the integrity of the piece even if the wool is not of high quality. If it is only slightly chemically washed, the heavy coarsely woven rug may have great durability. If the pile is too short, spaces or pockmarks may appear on the surface of the nap; therefore, rug producers use longer pile threads with the larger knots of coarser carpets.

India, close-up, vegetal dyes. Lightly washed and durable.

India, close-up, vegetal dyes.

Knot Count

High knot count, or more knots per square inch, is a good indicator of quality, particularly in formal, floral carpets. Knot count is not as important in tribal and village weavings, which are not judged by opulence and artistic beauty, but by artistic beauty alone.

Good detail, a very important aspect of quality in city workshop carpets, is generally associated with a high knot count. The more knots, the greater the detail, and the more labor required to produce the rug. Very fine rugs require highly skilled weavers as perfect execution of the complex graph or order of colors is extremely difficult. Knots may be counted by adding the number of nubs on the back of the rug in one inch running horizontally and one inch ver-tically and multiplying. A knot count of about 150 knots or more per square inch is considered fine. If one has the budget for the extra fine rug with 300 to 400 knots per square inch, in wool or silk from any major rug producing area, one will almost certainly be making an excellent rug investment if the carpet is flawless and well bought.

China, close-up, chrome dyes. Wool with silk highlights. Delicate spiral arabesques, high knot count.

Pakistan, close-up, vegetal dyes. About 300 knots per inch.

Wool

Soft wool is generally the best indicator of better quality but softness is not always correlated with high quality. Some wools are treated to feel soft, and, for example, inexpensive and finely machine spun Pakistan Bokara single wefted rugs may not wear as well as rugs made with rougher wools.

Inferior, inelastic tannery wool from dead sheep may be difficult to detect in carpets and bleached wool may be dry and brittle. Rugs that are made of tannery or bleached wool will not wear well over time.

Although one can sometimes sense the relative dryness of antique-washed wool, some chemically washed rugs will begin to wear in a few years and others will last many years. The amount of lanolin or protein loss from chemical washing remains unknown in these carpets. Therefore, rug rotation and padding have become necessities to add to the life of these carpets. Reputable rug retailers will only carry carpets whose wool is durable and strong.

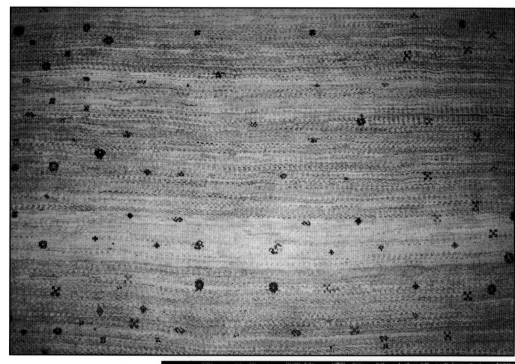

Iran, close-up, vegetal dyes. Wool warp and weft. Long wearing undyed wool with charming small accents.

Iran, close-up, vegetal dyes. Long, soft, and lustrous wool.

Who would have suspected that Persian Sarouk carpets, about sixty to eighty years old, were virtually indestructible because of their wool quality? Old Sarouk carpets, painted red when new, in the United States over many years were subsequently stripped back to a salmon color in the 1970s. They were then exported to Germany, where they now sit in many people's homes, still in perfect pile until this day! Wool pile rugs generally have great durability and resilience as they spring back into shape after being compressed by footsteps. Many people correctly take great pride in rugs that do not wear out over time but remain in excellent condition after many years of hard use.

India, close-up, chrome dyes. Old Persian Sarouk design.

Wool, the most important material in carpets, has surprisingly not attracted much interest or concern in the old carpet wholesale trade. Wool in old carpets is usually quite good and old carpet dealers were always more interested in the overall condition of a rug and its local origin rather than the softness of the wool. It was known, however, that some of the best old rugs, such as Mohtesham and Manchester Kashans from Iran, had softer wool.

Nepal, close-up, chrome dyes. Soft, excellent wool quality.

17

Like wool quality, dyes also cannot be rated for quality when purchased at retail. One must assume that the quality of dyes, like the quality of wool, is quite good today. Certain rugs, such as low grade Chinese hand-carved carpets, lose color when commercially washed, but most new carpets from about $30 a foot at retail wash surprisingly well even when originally chemically washed. The extent to which chemical washing reduces the adherence of dyes to wool also remains unknown. Only time will tell if dyes and wool are truly durable, but reports from commercial carpet cleaners are very encouraging.

Infrequent commercial cleanings are also a good idea because the knots and foundation of new antique-washed carpets have already been slightly unsettled by the chemical wash. Commercial cleaning may also be delayed because chemically washed rugs with vegetal or synthetic chrome dyes are less susceptible to moth damage than lightly soap-washed, vegetal-dyed rugs of yesteryear. Old synthetically dyed carpets rarely suffer from the ravages of moths whereas moths have been a great problem in old vegetal-dyed rugs that were not chemically washed.

Chrome dyes allow for more color variety and since 1950 do not seem to show signs of wool damage or oxidization. Chrome dyes may fade too little or too evenly, as opposed to the differential rates of pleasant fading of different vegetal dyes, over time. While vegetal dyes are color fast, synthetic chrome dyes fuse into wool better and are less likely to run or bleed into one another. In the old rug trade, vegetal-dyed blues and reds sometimes ran into ivory or white colored wool and the fugitive dyes had to be bleached out with chemicals.

Vegetal dyes have the advantage of being more organic, which adds earthiness to carpets. Carpets that are vegetal-dyed are often made the old fashioned

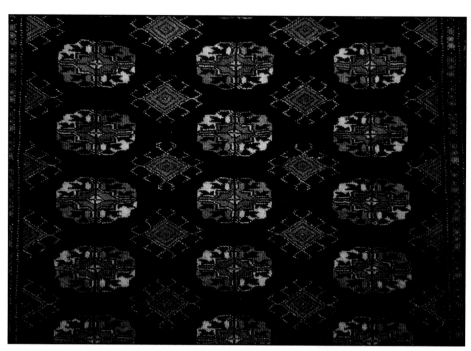

Pakistan Bokara, close-up, chrome dyes.

Iranian soumak flatweave, close-up. Vegetal dyes, and embroidered pile.

way and combined with hand-spun yarn yield a desirable natural or non-machine assisted quality to carpets. Vegetal-dyed rugs are often made in exactly the same way as rugs used to be made hundreds of years ago—an advantage that modern, high quality furniture makers who rely upon machines must surely envy.

Vegetal dyes have a beautiful, lively quality that is warm and cheerful. All of the greatest old rugs of the past were vegetal-dyed. Antique-washed, vegetal-dyed rugs do not require a very strong wash, thus preserving the essential oils in the wool pile and cotton foundation. The patina that can be achieved with a vegetal-dyed rug that is antique-washed is generally superior to the patina of the chrome-dyed rug.

Historically, collectors have only been interested in vegetal-dyed carpets. If one synthetic dye is suspected in an old Turkoman or Turkish tribal or village rug, the rug is invalidated as a collectible. If a synthetic dye is present, the rug was also probably woven by a different tribe or in a different village from where it was originally woven for many years. Although some new vegetal-dyed rugs employ synthetic indigo, which may even be a foundation for green or violet, this will probably be acceptable to future collectors of these carpets. The reason future collectors will have to be more tolerant of a synthetic dye is that new vegetal-dyed rugs will be judged by their beauty, definition, flow, and contrast rather than by whether they contain one or more lab-produced dyes. Today's synthetic chrome-dyed rugs, vastly superior to early synthetic-dyed rugs, are probably just as likely to retain value in the future as vegetal-dyed rugs.

Iran, close-up, vegetal dyes. Cheerful, lively colors.

Abrash

Abrash, or hue change within individual colors, has become one of the most important elements in the evaluation of carpet quality today. Old carpet wholesalers never spent much time talking about good abrash in the past, but only bad abrash.

Bad abrash was sometimes caused by inferior wool used in different areas of a carpet that did not hold the dye as well as better wool found in other parts of a rug. Bad abrash was a sudden change within a particular color that caused the color to stand out too much against other colors and designs. Rugs with this problem were always very hard to resell in the old carpet market and dealers assiduously avoided buying rugs with bad abrash. Good abrash is always subtle, graduated, harmonious, and does not attract too much attention to itself. Dramatic or contrasting abrash is more acceptable in contemporary than antique carpets.

Rugs may now be evaluated according to the elegance of the flow of the abrash. Not only vegetal-dyed, but also chrome-dyed carpets exhibit the beauty, brilliance, and depth of abrash.

Abrash, in general, cannot compensate for the other important attributes of carpet quality or beauty, but may be considered a way to enhance the harmony, warmth, and flow of other colors and designs. Sometimes, however, strikingly beautiful abrash may make a rug with a questionable design quite acceptable to the connoisseur. Abrash adds life to carpets that may have been dulled or weakened by the regimentation of commercialization.

Now the harmony of the abrash must be analyzed along with the shape and flow of the designs within the carpet. The great importance of the beauty of grain in wood furniture parallels the increased significance of the beauty of abrash in new carpets. Wood grain and abrash are of equal importance in analyzing the quality of furniture and carpets today.

Pakistan, close-up, vegetal dyes. Fairly subtle abrash or color variation.

Iran, close-up, vegetal dyes. Dramatic abrash or color variation in fine carpet.

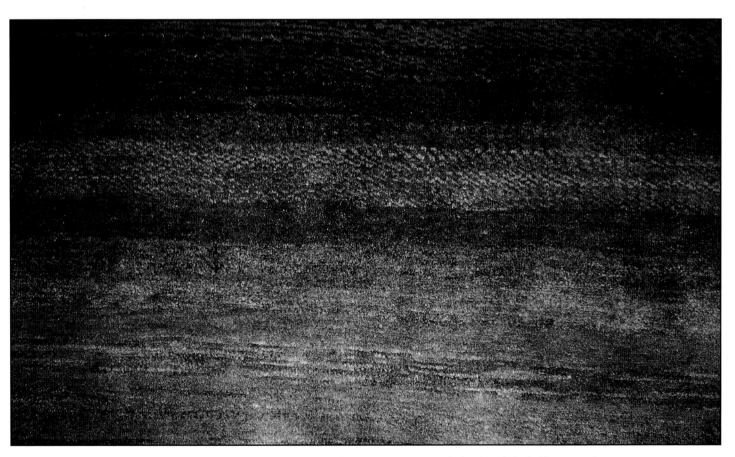

Iran, close-up, vegetal dyes. Wool warp and weft. Abrash or color variation in original village weaving.

Local Interest

Local interest in the Oriental rug is a small area of the carpet which will always capture the imagination and is a feast for the senses. Good rugs generally have a lot of local interest.

When examining a carpet, the buyer should try to see if local interest is sufficiently present, such that the rug will not become boring over time. Many European buyers will examine rugs very closely for local interest to see which of the last two finalist carpets is the most interesting and beautiful. One rug may have a slightly better main border or guard border which may tip the scales toward the purchase of that particular carpet.

Pakistan, close-up, vegetal dyes. Good local interest within sets of designs.

Iranian soumak flatweave, close-up. Vegetal dyes, and embroidered pile. Good local interest.

Nepalese rugs with simple designs may still have a lot of local interest if the solid field color is exquisite and sufficiently variegated with abrash or color shadings. A single-colored or self-toned rug with many different, glorious shadings that may have a lot of local interest, even if it does not have any design at all.

Nepal, close-up, chrome dyes. Local interest in subtle abrash or color variation.

Flow

Flow is an important aspect of rug aesthetics. Designs should harmoniously blend into one another in an elegant manner without interruption. Flow may be interrupted by a garish color or a peculiar design that does not seem to complement the rest of the rug. Strong designs may be disturbing and more powerful designs should harmonize with smaller and softer designs into an orderly whole.

Most old classical designs had good flow which was improved, historically, by trade with the West. The American public has always preferred harmonious rugs to blend with surrounding fabrics in large homes.

Sometimes successful flow is in the eye of the beholder. Some people may find that an innovated design flows successfully whereas others might be disturbed by a sense of arrested flow in certain areas. Classically oriented rug connoisseurs find it difficult to accept new designs that do not have historical precedent because the flow is often slightly arrested by the new designs.

Iran, close-up, vegetal dyes. Good flow in elegant layered arabesques.

India, close-up, vegetal dyes. Good flow and proportion between large and small motifs.

24

Spacing

Each design has a sharp line which separates it from the surrounding space. Space is not irrelevant, but the highly significant color substance within which designs are stretched. Rugs may be judged as much by their spaces as by their designs and colors. Early court rugs are dated by the amount of space surrounding the motifs and older carpets often have more space, which prevents clutter.

Old Turkoman rugs are also judged by spaces which surround designs. If the space is too small, disorder and confusion may result, thus dating the rug to a later point in time, and degenerating the entire carpet. As in classical and other kinds of music, when a note is held, a space results that balances the entire composition.

In very fine and detailed old or new floral rugs, more space may successfully be filled with design, but again, colors and designs must be true and clear. The idea is to attain design complexity without confusion. Color complementarity is important in very fine rugs to prevent them from having designs that are too busy. One wrong color can throw off the entire effect. Paisley shawls exemplify the effect that these rugs attempt to achieve.

India, close-up, chrome dyes. Pleasant open space between designs.

Space between designs is most important. In general, Tibetan and classical Chinese rugs have the most space, Indian and Turkish rugs have less space, and Persian rugs have the least space.

Space adds power and majesty to designs and open field designs are often more elegant then full field designs. Full field designs are most elegant when motifs and colors form an integrated and harmonious totality in which no design or color stands out too much against the background. The predominantly solid color of the more open field design with little surface ornamentation often allows for greater flexibility in matching adjacent fabrication.

Nepal, close-up, chrome dyes. Simplicity, open space, and economy of color.

Borders

The narrow guard borders that surround the main border of the carpet contain one of the most important keys to the quality of the carpet. Rug connoisseurs and savvy retail buyers always check the guard borders in traditional carpets to see if the designs are well defined and the colors are pure. If the major, or even narrower, minor guard borders are dull, flat or uninteresting, a carpet will probably not be of very fine quality.

India, close-up, probably chrome dyes. Excellent design definition in major and minor borders.

The large main borders should contrast the main field but should also harmonize with the main field by picking up some colors. Buyers should check to see that the borders are complementary and do not look like they belong on another carpet. At the same time, the main border should not overly harmonize with the main field.

Pakistan, close-up, vegetal dyes. Contrast and harmony between borders and main field.

The borders should be differentiated from the main field to add variety to the carpet. The exceptions are antique-washed, unusual, and very fine, well-crafted carpets in which the connoisseur is more forgiving and accepts overly harmonious borders.

China, close-up, chrome dyes. Fine weave and crisp, innovative border design.

Fringes

Fringes are the ends of the vertical warp foundation threads which run lengthwise and form the loom upon which the carpet is woven. They are not superficial end threads sewn onto the carpet for good or bad looks. Many clients do not like fringes because they are too light and apt to soil and only want rugs without fringes. This severely limits their choices and, coupled with the need to match fabrics, often creates an untenable situation for buyers and salespersons.

Pakistan, close-up, vegetal dyes. Perfectly acceptable light colored fringes, well bound.

People should tolerate fringes because they are found in the vast majority of carpets. When tightly bound at the ends, fringes protect the rug from losing valuable pile. All rugs that are well bound at the ends are securely closed; however, long fringes are slightly better than short because they do not wear out as fast.

Many weavers traditionally cut the fringes short and cannot be changed from this habit by the headman of the village or the importer. Also, producers may prefer short fringes since they are usually found in antique rugs.

Pakistan, close-up, chrome dyes. Good quality, fairly long, well-braided fringes.

Reproduction & Innovation

Good design reproduction is a very important part of rug quality. Unfortunately, too many new rug producers, with an inadequate knowledge of old rugs, attempt, but fail, to innovate or add new designs successfully. Weird designs may result that are oversimplifications of classic old designs. Or, a strange design may have no precedent in old classic carpets and is not very elegant. Educated new rug buyers should study old rug books to get a sense of what the great old designs of the past looked like.

Chinese silk, close-up of center medallion, chrome dyes. Successful combination of tradition and innovation.

It is safer for new rug producers to make exact reproductions of the designs of the old classics, changing the colors only. Some of the greatest carpet designers today have good knowledge of antique carpets and reproduce old rugs to their exact original specifications. Assuming that the prototype is a great and well-proportioned rug, the exact reproduction assures the correct proportionality found in the original. The "original" was, of course, directly or indirectly derived from still earlier sources.

Some of the best reproductions are "foolers" that experts occasionally, mistakenly believe are real antiques. Every year, a few knowledgeable old rug dealers will pay very high prices at auction for the "foolers" that they believe are rare old carpets.

Turkey, close-up, vegetal dyes. A close reproduction of an old, probably northwest Persian design.

Carpet buyers should consider buying more new geometric designed rugs which are often easier to successfully reproduce than new formal floral-designed carpets. New Nepalese rugs exemplify this fact. Good new carpet salespersons should be able to help the retail buyer find a successfully reproduced or innovated geometric or floral carpet.

Nepal, close-up, chrome dyes, mixed weave. Innovation of geometric modern abstract design.

Innovation in new rug designs and colors is a good idea if done correctly. Innovation is good because it is an antidote to commercialization in carpets. Too many new rugs are run-of-the-mill or too dull and distinctive rugs may consequently be good investments. New designs introduced into reproductions of old rugs must be elegant and merge into the older classical designs. When this is done successfully, a superb and perhaps collectible rug may result.

Only a few producers of new rugs have the great knowledge and artistic ability to create a beautifully innovated carpet in which all of the new designs or colors blend with the rest of the carpet into an integrated and harmonious whole. The genius of innovative designers often lies in the fact that they exactly reproduce the colors and designs of the old masters and do not innovate at all. Their sagacity abides in their humility and the respect and admiration that they have for their perceptive predecessors.

China, close-up of center medallion. Effective innovation of old Persian design.

Commercialization

The Oriental carpet trade today is so commercialized that only beauty and quality can compensate for the effects of commerce. Because of commercialism, Oriental carpets have lost much more of their Eastern spirit than in earlier days.

In prior times, commercialization was more peripheral and was ameliorated by local endemic cultural traditions in the East which maintained a degree of Eastern spirituality in carpets.

Nonetheless, Oriental carpet scholars who wrote books eighty years ago lamented the growth of commercialism at that time as well.

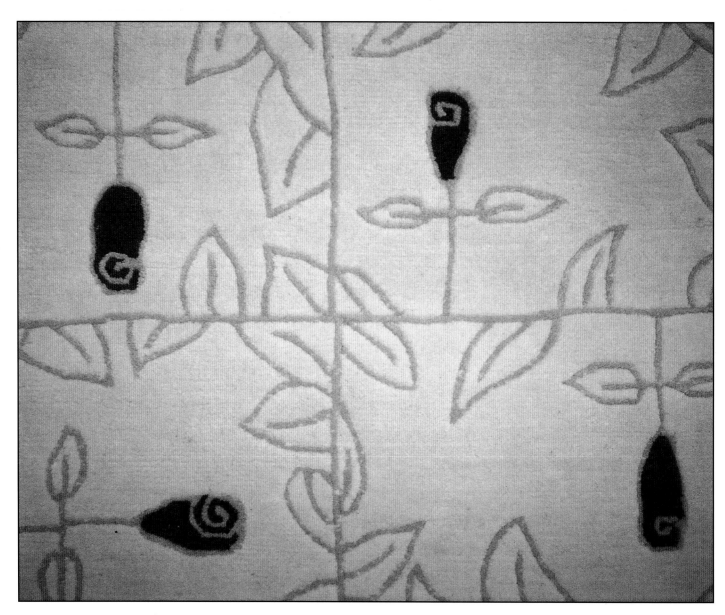

Nepal, close-up, chrome dyes. Highly commercialized, yet original fusion of East and West.

Some rug producers are trying to revitalize the Eastern spirit by allowing village weavers to express themselves more in their weavings with whimsical expressions of individual, rather than group, creativity. Vegetal-dyed rugs are an attempt to reproduce the sense that was conveyed by the great rugs of the nineteenth century and earlier, which were not woven expressly for export but for home use, home use and barter, or occasional export.

Antique or chemical washing represents an attempt to reproduce great old rugs as closely as possible. Antique washing attempts to reverse the ill effects of commercialization by capturing the patina and harmony of great old rugs whose colors have naturally harmonized through exposure to light, wear, and commercial washing. This explains the continuing allure of the Oriental rug in the era of the modern home.

Iran, close-up, vegetal dyes. Eastern village or tribal revival.

Rugs today may be commercialized but still convey, in differing degrees, a taste of the culture of the East. Knowledgeable rug producers are attempting to reproduce the old, less commercialized carpets in more harmonious color palettes which still convey, in some small but not insignificant way, the glory, power, and majesty of Eastern peasant culture and refined Islamic civilization.

In a supreme irony, some of the most highly coveted antique Persian Tabriz, Mahal, and Heriz, as well as antique Turkish Oushak and Indian Agra carpets, which may sell for hundreds of thousands of dollars today, were highly commercialized carpets woven for export. Producers of carpets today may take heart and be more optimistic about the future of their rugs in the light of this fact.

China, close-up of center medallion, chrome dyes.

Unusual Rugs

In today's highly commercialized rug environment, in which the importance of local pedigree is reduced, unusual rugs may be better investments. Too many rugs are run-of-the-mill because of excessive design harmony thus increasing the value of the unusual in today's market.

India, close-up, vegetal dyes. Unusual rug with design derived from old fabric.

Nepal, close-up, chrome dyes, wool and silk. Novel and distinctive.

Since unusual rugs generally have strong, dominant designs and colors, adjacent fabrics must be softer to accommodate them. Furniture may be placed on top of these unique and desirable carpets to soften the blow of busy designs and colors. In the old rug trade, unusual rugs that could not be pigeonholed into the appropriate village, town, or country usually were readily resold in time. Some premier old carpet retailers would look for distinctive, unprecedented rugs for which they could ask higher prices. The lack of pedigree may ironically have been an advantage in the sense that the carpet was rare or unique and consequently difficult to appraise in the standard way.

A rug, however, must not simply be unique, but also elegant, well crafted, and beautiful. An exceptional rug, which does not look like it was woven either in Europe or the East may have the value that the owner believes that it has rather than a known market value. The beautiful rug of unknown provenance from any age may have a value that can vary from, for example, $5000 to $50,000 depending upon the dealer that was presenting it.

An unusual rug should not be confused with a so-called "bastard" carpet. The "bastard" rug is one that is reminiscent of the pedigreed carpet but contains changes that detract rather than add to the rug's overall beauty. For example, a rug may have a classical field design associated with a particular area but a weird border. The good unusual rug, on the other hand, is one that is different enough from known rugs with pedigree that it attains a stature of its own and is not judged by its relationship to other known or distinguishable rugs.

Chinese silk, close-up, chrome dyes. Silk warp and weft. Bold and imaginative.

Design Versus Color

Color in carpets gained importance relative to design in recent years. Color has always been the royal road to Oriental carpet appreciation. Design was very important in early court rugs of the seventeenth century as well as later old rugs of the nineteenth century. Scholars analyzed designs to see from whence they were derived. Some sources of designs found in carpets were previously seen in other media such as pottery, textiles, tile work, and architecture from other lands. For the connoisseur, design will always be at least as important as color in carpets.

Color gained importance with the growth of the decorative rug, as well as the architect C.F.A. Voysey's simple carpets with magnificent colors, in the early twentieth century. The old, early twentieth century Turkish Oushak, Persian Mahal, and Tabriz are decorative carpets whose beautiful soft red, rust, and ivory colors tended to outweigh their designs in significance.

Nepal, close-up, chrome dyes. Color dominant rug.

China, close-up, chrome dyes, silk highlights. Design dominant rug.

Today the growth of chemical washing vegetal and synthetic chrome-dyed rugs, both in more ornate traditional as well as simple and pure Nepalese carpets, has tended to also increase the importance of color over design.

India, close-up, vegetal and chrome dyes. Color dominant rug.

Red, Blue & Ivory

Red in various manifestations is the most important color in Oriental carpets. Red may vary in intensity from a pale rust or brick to a deep, rich vermillion or scarlet. A good beginner's classical rug might be predominantly red in order to get a sense of a color found to be dominant in so many of the great rugs of the past. If the design and overall quality of the rug is good, one usually cannot go far wrong with a traditional or decorative red or rust-colored rug.

The second most important color in rugs, generally shied away from by so many Americans for its obtrusiveness and lack of adaptability to fabric, is blue. Whereas red is the most highly coveted color historically in Turkish rugs, dark, midnight blue, or blue black is the most treasured color in Persian rugs. Dark blue may be the best background color because it adds definition to the surface designs that lie upon it.

The third most important color from undyed sheep's wool is ivory or white, which most successfully appears in conjunction with red and blue. A rug with red or rust, blue, and ivory has the advantage of containing three colors with the greatest pedigree in the old carpet trade.

Old ivory-colored rugs from the Caucusus and Iran were often more highly coveted by old rug dealers because ivory is also a perfect background for designs of great precision and beauty. New classical rug producers should make more ivory, off white, or white-colored rugs, because, like dark blue, these colors add power to the surface designs of a carpet. Ivory also conveys a sense of age to a carpet without the necessity of chemical washing to reduce color intensity.

Pakistan, close-up, vegetal dyes. Classical red-rust, blue, and ivory colors.

India, close-up, vegetal dyes. Classical rust, blue, and ivory colors.

The most important design in new rugs is the Lotus, Shah Abbas, or Palmette. Historically, it is also the most notable design, particularly in the early Isfahan Vase carpets. Its only rival for design supremacy was the hunting scene pattern, which has hunters on horseback or felines in combat.

The Lotus design may vary significantly in shape and size but is usually a large, flat, serrated or rounded leaf viewed from the side or top. It may be square and angular, or long, narrow, and curvilinear. One rug may contain four or five variations of this design, each quite distinct from the other. The reason for the variation is because the Lotus has a round lily at the base, a flower sprouting upwards, and buds in various stages of development.

When properly drafted and executed, it is the most elegant design in Oriental carpets today. Active carpet retailers cannot get enough pieces with this variegated design, which works so well with vines, peonies, tulips, and other flowers and motifs. This design probably accounts for over fifty percent of curvilinear and stylized floral Persian inspired city carpets from India and Pakistan today. It is also prevalent in geometric designed village carpets.

What accounts for the exceptional popularity of carpets employing this design which never decreases from year to year? The Lotus design seems to convey more of the Middle Eastern spirit than other designs and has a calming effect upon the overall flow of smaller motifs while adding power, *gravitas*, and local interest to the carpet. By increasing the scale of the design it reduces busyness while not standing out too much against other smaller ornaments. It breaks up the monotony while not disrupting the integration necessary for the total simultaneous perception of the composition.

The eye moves from the large scaled leaf to the smaller flowers and buds of the Lotus and the visual pleasure results from the flow between distinctive sets of designs including, of course, other floral motifs. In this way the viewer experiences the warmth of differing shapes of color draped against a solid background color, an experience not unlike the encounter one might have when viewing an early court carpet in a museum with very complex layers of designs.

Without the Lotus, the rug experience would diminish into the total main effect of the simultaneous perception of small flowers and leaves only. The eye stops roving and focuses upon the Lotus leaf or flower after initially perceiving the rug in its entirety. Now the eye can find repose in this broad plant form. Actually, the Lotus takes the viewer by the hand through the rug experience the easy way by compelling the viewer to go beyond the initial overall impression into the classic rug adventure, if only briefly. The Lotus motif is particularly elegant on a dark blue background and is usually found in the desirable all over design which is easier to center in a room.

In its more stylized or geometric manifestation, the large Lotus leaf may expand into the spacious Shield Palmette, which may be found in old Heriz and Bakshiash and new Heriz and Bakshiash inspired carpets. Sometimes the Lotus flower may become more rounded and abstract and evolve into an undulating lozenge or amoeba-like structure found in certain old Bidjar and new Bidjar inspired carpets. Suffice to say, this compound design is found in an extremely large number of permutations and combinations, or guises and disguises.

As with so many other designs, experts and laypersons may debate whether a motif is a Lotus leaf, flower, or bud, or whether indeed a Lotus in any of its forms is the same as a Palmette or Shah Abbas design. To complicate matters further, a Lotus may have an unusual shape or abstract form which is hard to derive from the plant or which may look similar to another design.

Pakistan, close-up, vegetal dyes. Lotus leaves in soft, decorative rug.

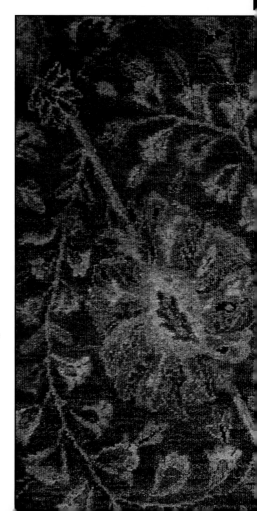

India, close-up, vegetal dyes. Lotus
leaves and branches with small leaves
and flowers.

Designs evolve through the experimentation of designers in the East or West who attempt to modulate the Lotus by making it larger or smaller. Some vegetable-dyed rugs from India have extra large and dramatic geometric Lotus leaves, with the central fruits superimposed, which work quite successfully with the proper color complementarity.

If the Lotus in any of its aspects is large, and either serrated or rounded, it is usually more amenable to contemporary decor than the smaller, more classical and curvilinear forms which are embedded in a more intricately detailed design. The great popularity of the Lotus may be in large part due to its adaptability to either traditional or modern settings depending upon the size and shape of the motif.

India, close-up, vegetal dyes. Extra large lotus leaves and branches with small leaves and flowers.

When viewed from above, Lotus flower petals peel away from central fruits or cone-like shoots which come up from the core. The small circles in the center represent the hub of the flower when the viewer looks down into the plant. The Lotus flower from a bird's-eye view may be rounded or crenellated or may even look like a starfish. Sometimes a small Lotus flower viewed from above is actually a rosette and this ambiguity is difficult to resolve.

Pakistan, close-up, vegetal dyes. Lotus leaves, connecting arabesques, and small, circular lotus flowers.

Chapter Two
Rug Weaving Areas —————————

India

India produces thick, heavy, very good quality rugs today in low, middle, and high price points. The finish is generally quite good and the cotton foundation threads are thick and tightly plied together. The wool pile tends to be long which increases the longevity of the carpet, even if the wool quality is not always the best. Indian wool is good and is sometimes mixed with New Zealand wool to produce better quality and a softer nap.

The Western importer has encouraged the Indian producers to soften the colors and harmonize them for the Western market. This has been the most revolutionary development in Oriental carpets in the last twenty years. The Indian style is a beautiful, more rectilinear interpretation of old curvilinear, heavily ornamented, full field designs from Iran.

Indian designs are delicate, angular or geometric, with a good deal of space surrounding the motifs. The greater space enhances the designs and adds elegance to the carpet.

There are several very important producers in India today that are creating designs and color palettes that are among the best in the industry. Each of the best workshops has that inimitable quality that distinguishes it from another and gives the carpets the pedigree required to achieve and maintain enduring value.

Many Indian rugs are made with vegetal dyes from natural sources such as madder and indigo roots, nut husks, and tree bark.

India, close-up, chrome dyes. Medium grade with well spaced ornamentation.

Opposite page: India, close-up, vegetal dyes. Heavy, durable, and lightly washed, with bright and fresh top colors.

India, vegetal dyes, hunting scene design, 4' x 7'. Estimated value $2,500.

India, vegetal dyes, large serrated leaf design, 6' x 9'. Estimated value $4,500.

India, probably vegetal and chrome dyes, 8' x 10'. Estimated value $4,700.

India, chrome dyes, 6' x 9'. Estimated value $1,700.

India, vegetal dyes, 8' x 10'. Estimated value $6,500.

India, vegetal dyes. Lattice and tree-of-life designs, 8' x 10'. Estimated value $6,500.

India, chrome dyes, fine hunting scene design, 8.6' x 16'. Estimated value $10,500.

India, vegetal dyes. Center medallion design, sumptuous colors, 9' x 13'. Estimated value $9,500.

India, vegetal dyes, 9.6' x 18'.
Estimated value $14,000.

India, vegetal dyes, 8.6' x 12'. Estimated value $8,300.

India, vegetal dyes, 6' x 9'.
Estimated value $4,500.

India, vegetal dyes, 8' x 10'. Estimated value $6,500.

India, vegetal dyes, serrated leaf border, 4.6' x 7'. Estimated value $2,600.

India, vegetal dyes, cloud band border, 9' x 12'. Estimated value $8,800.

India, vegetal dyes. Striking abrash or color changes, 9' x 12'. Estimated value $7,800.

India, vegetal dyes, 9' x 12'. Estimated value $8,800.

India, vegetal dyes, tree-of-life design, 8' x 10'. Estimated value $5,800.

India, vegetal dyes. Lotus or palmette design, 9' x 12'. Estimated value $8,800.

India, vegetal dyes. Herati or serrated leaf surrounding rosette design, 10' x 10'. Estimated value $4,500.

India, vegetal dyes, 9' x 12'. Asymmetrical main field design adds informality. Estimated value $8,800.

India, vegetal dyes. Tree-of-life and prayer designs, 2' 6" x 6'. Estimated value $1,200.

India, probably vegetal dyes. Cloud bands and layered designs, 9' x 12'. Estimated value $5,000.

India, vegetal dyes, center medallion design, 9' x 12'. Estimated value. $8,800.

India, probably chrome dyes, good, balanced abrash, 9' x 12'. Estimated value $3,500.

India, vegetal dyes. Garden, compartment, and tree-of-life designs, 9' x 12'. Estimated value $8,800.

India, vegetal dyes. Tree-of-life and prayer designs, repeating cartouche border, 3' x 5'. Estimated value $750.

India, vegetal dyes, good, vivid colors, 9' x 12'. Estimated value $5,000.

India, vegetal dyes. Vibrant abrash, serrated leaf and informal prayer designs, 6' x 9'. Estimated value $4,000.

India, vegetal dyes, center medallion design, 6' x 9'. Estimated value $4,000.

India, vegetal dyes. Swirling arabesque or stylized vine design, 9' x 12'. Estimated value $8,800.

India, vegetal dyes. Lotus or palmette, cloud band, and arabesque designs, 9' x 12'. Estimated value $7,500.

India, probably vegetal and chrome dyes. Highly detailed and opulent, in the court style, 10' x 14'. Estimated value $11,500.

India, vegetal dyes, 9' x 12'. Estimated value $8,800.

India, vegetal dyes. Compartment, tree-of-life, and prayer designs, 7' x 12'. Estimated value $7,000.

India, vegetal dyes. Lotus or palmette designs, repeating cartouche border with small cloud bands, 8' x 10'. Estimated value $6,500.

India, vegetal dyes, 9' x 12'. Estimated value $7,800.

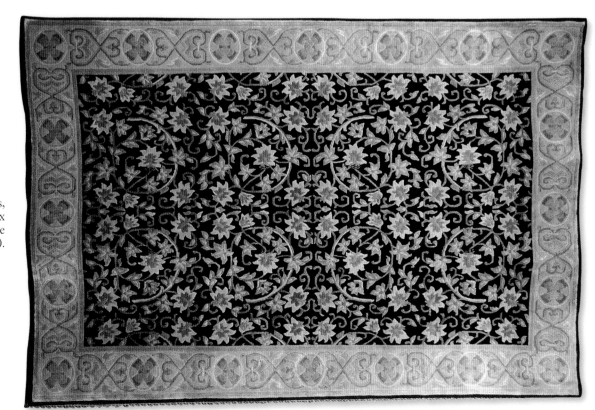

India, chrome dyes, Tibetan design, 6' x 9'. Estimated value $1,500.

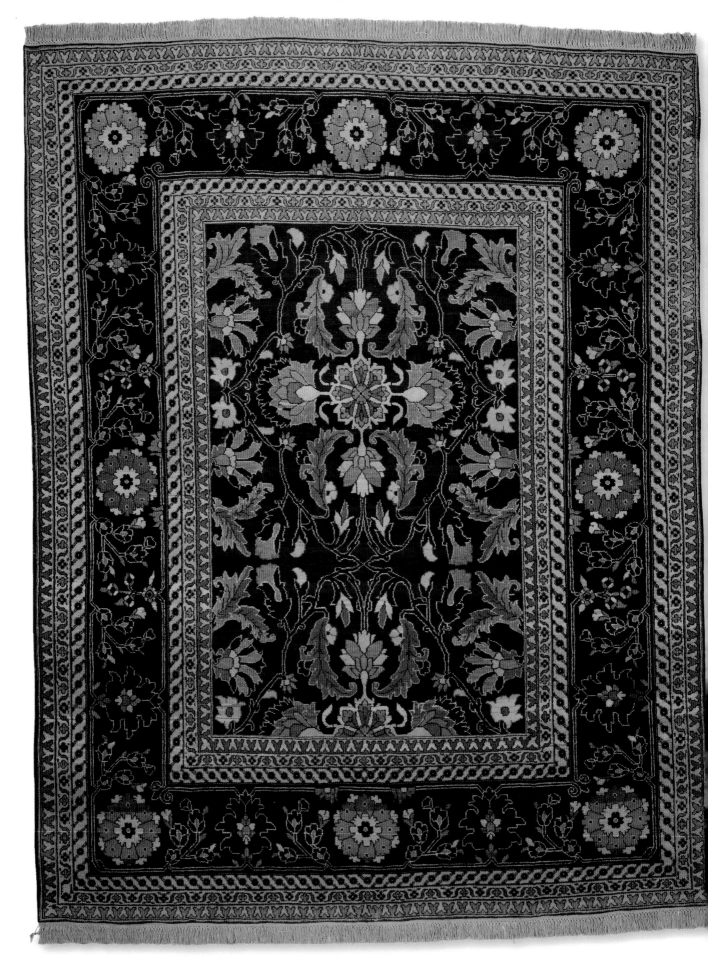

India, probably vegetal and chrome dyes, 8' x 10'. Estimated value $3,600.

India, chrome dyes, 8' x 10'. Estimated value
$3,300.

India, chrome dyes.
Tibetan and modern
abstract designs, 6' x
9'. Estimated value
$1,500.

Pakistan

Pakistani rugs are the great rival of Indian rugs today. In general, they have a shorter pile but stiffer, harder, and more tightly twisted foundation threads than Indian rugs. One is in uncharted waters when analyzing Pakistani rugs in the sense that they had no pedigree in the old rug trade of the past. Before the division of India and the formation of Pakistan, India did produce a few distinctive types of old rugs with pedigree such as the Agra and Amritsar.

One may argue that Pakistan is producing the best rugs today in the medium and high price points and pedigree is beginning to develop in the finer qualities or better workshops. Very fine chrome-dyed Pakistani rugs in classical Persian designs have a similar feel to new Persian rugs but the designs are more harmonious.

Pakistan, close-up, vegetal dyes.

The finest quality Pakistani vegetal-dyed rugs combine elegance, opulence, and antique patina into an integrated whole in what is arguably the best wool rug produced today. The medium grade vegetal-dyed, antique-washed Pakistani rugs that go under several names, including "Khyber" and "Peshawar," have revolutionized the industry and are now probably the most popular traditional handmade rugs in geometric designs being sold worldwide. They perfectly replicate the look and feel of highly coveted antique Persian Mahals and Turkish Oushaks, and while they may not be collectible, they blend so easily and look so beautiful that they sell at a very fast pace. The fact that so many people react so well to Khyber carpets indicates that the taste for old carpets continues today with these incredible reproductions or "gentle Orientals".

Pakistan, close-up, vegetal dyes. Alluring color, granular texture, and antique patina.

The traditional classic repeat medallion Pakistani "Princess Bokara" has been an American favorite for many years. It is perhaps the most inexpensive handmade pile rug and retails for about $18 a square foot. Heavier or thicker quality Pakistani Bokaras may cost a little more at retail. The repeat elephant hoof medallions cover the surface of all variety of solid background colors including crimson, emerald green, beige, salmon, and black.

Pakistan, close-up, chrome dyes. Bokara design.

Because Pakistani Bokaras have low wool density, they do not last as long as other heavier carpets. However, they are usually the first choice of the novice rug buyer and go with a large assortment of fabrics. They always add a nice touch of old world elegance to the home. Because they are thin, lightweight, and portable, they are also the first choice of South American tourists who buy them on their visits to the United States. While Pakistani Bokara rugs have no collectible value, the simplicity and precision of their pure understated designs, so reminiscent of the great old Turkoman rugs of the past, also explains their popularity.

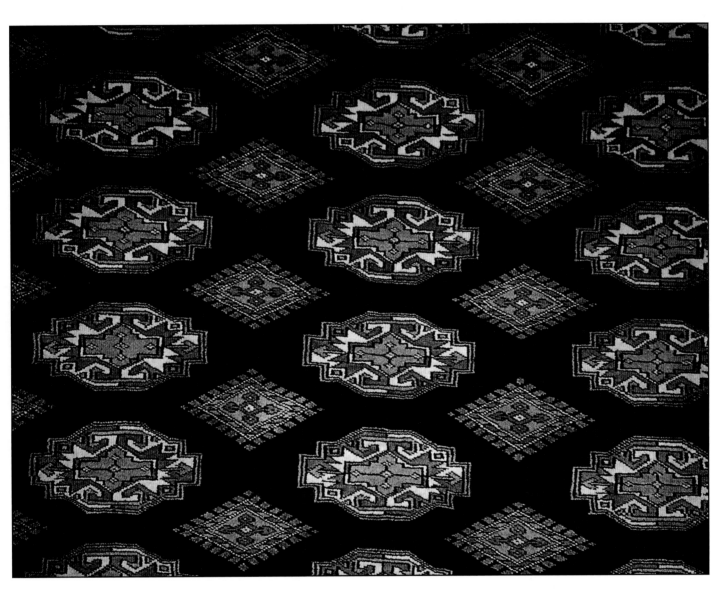

Pakistan, close-up, chrome dyes. Bokara design.

Pakistan, probably vegetal and chrome dyes. Fine weave, good detail and definition, 9' x 12'. Estimated value $10,000.

Pakistan, probably vegetal and chrome dyes, 9' x 12'. Satisfactory main field asymmetry. Estimated value $4,500.

Pakistan, probably vegetal and chrome dyes. Lotus or palmette design, well spaced, 6' x 9'. Estimated value $2,200.

Pakistan, probably vegetal and chrome dyes. The "gentle Oriental", 9' x 12'. Estimated value $3,700.

Pakistan, probably vegetal and chrome dyes, 9' x 12'. Estimated value $4,500.

Pakistan, vegetal dyes. Red and green top colors, 8' x 10'. Estimated value $3,300.

Pakistan, chrome dyes, 8' x 8'. Estimated value $2,200.

Pakistan, chrome dyes. Repeating cloud bands in border, 8' x 11'. Estimated value $3,600.

Pakistan, vegetal dyes. Economy of color and design, good spacing between motifs, 8' x 10'. Estimated value $3,300.

Pakistan, probably chrome dyes, 9' x 12'. Estimated value $4,500.

Pakistan, vegetal dyes, 8' x 10'. Estimated value $2,700.

Pakistan, vegetal dyes. Large geometric herati or serrated leaf surrounding rosette design, 8' x 10'. Estimated value $2,700.

Pakistan, vegetal dyes. Vital colors in close reproduction of old Caucasian Kazak rug, 4.6' x 5.6'. Estimated value $900.

Pakistan, vegetal dyes. Dynamic designs in close reproduction of old Caucasian Kazak rug, 4' x 6'. Estimated value $900.

Iran or Persia

Persian rugs, like Swiss watches, were always coveted for their quality and pedigree. Each village or city had a continuous tradition of weaving the same or similar designs for home use and export for hundreds of years. Kashan, Kerman, Bidjar, Tabriz, Heriz, and Mahal are some of the great old Persian rugs with pedigree.

Persian rugs were valuable because they were inimitable symbols of a particular village or town. They were and are a kind of currency that could be converted into liquid cash at any time. Pedigree or provenance assured tried and true quality and proven colors and designs in Persian rugs exported to the West over the past 100 years.

Iran is trying to win back the market in the United States that it lost during the embargo between 1986 and 2000 so the prices for most Persian rugs are quite cheap. The colors are lively, fresh, and crisp as Iranians have not, for the most part, mastered the art of harmonizing colors and antique washing for the Western market. Nonetheless, magnificent, lively, and cheerful colors, which represent the soul of the Oriental carpet craft, are combined beautifully in most Persian rugs today. They are a good investment for people who do not have to match their carpet to busy fabrics and can tolerate a degree of color disharmony.

The classic rugs from Kashan, Kerman, Tabriz, Mashad, Bidjar, and other cities of Iran, which have been weaving the same designs continuously for many years, are some the best examples of quality, elegance, proportion, symmetry, and style in the Oriental carpet craft. A home designed with formal or semi-formal rugs should have one red or dark blue Persian city rug in one room, if possible. The experience of a good Persian rug would be one of the best lessons that one can have on Oriental carpets without reading a book on the subject.

Iran, close-up, chrome dyes. Bidjar with center medallion and herati designs. Localized pedigree.

Iran, close-up, chrome dyes. Fine Tabriz with center medallion and herati designs. Localized pedigree.

There are now some producers in Iran that are adjusting colors and designs for the Western market with the aid of creative Western designers. These rugs, woven with vegetal dyes and handspun wool, and perfectly washed to integrate colors, are also among the best rugs woven today. They represent the perfect union of East and West in which vitality and temperance merge in rugs of consummate beauty and elegance.

Iran, close-up, vegetal dyes. Wool warp and weft. Renaissance of natural dying in Iran.

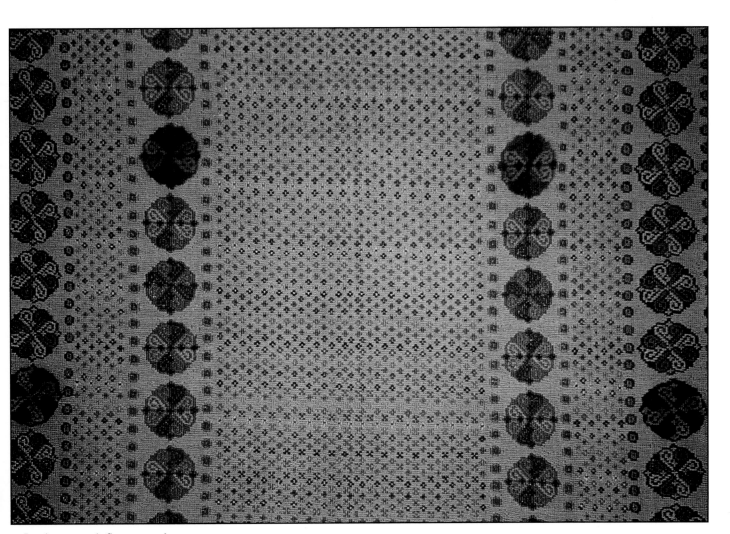

Iranian soumak flatweave, close-up.
Vegetal dyes and embroidered pile.

Iran, vegetal dyes. Closely resembles luxurious early Persian court carpets, 8' x 10'. Estimated value $11,000.

Iran, vegetal dyes. Old Persian vase design may be the most elegant ever drafted, 4' x 6'. Estimated value $3,500.

Iran, vegetal dyes. Crisp, powerful design with high definition, 9' x 13'. Estimated value $16,000.

Iranian village rug, vegetal dyes, 2.9' x 11'.
Estimated value $3,000.

Iranian village rug, vegetal dyes, 2.9' x 12'.
Estimated value $3,200.

Iran, vegetal dyes. Hunting scene design. Similar to regal early Persian court carpets, 8' x 10'. Estimated value $11,000.

Iran, vegetal dyes, beautiful green main field color, crisp, delicate design, 8' x 12'. Estimated value $13,000.

Iran, vegetal dyes. Hunting scene design with well-drawn animals, 8' x 12'. Estimated value $13,000.

Iran, vegetal dyes. Elegant and luxurious, 10' x 14'. Estimated value $19,000.

Iranian village rug, vegetal dyes. Wool warp and weft, 3' x 5'. Estimated value $1,500.

Iranian village rug, vegetal dyes. Wool warp and weft, 4' x 7'. Estimated value $3,000.

Iran, vegetal dyes. Magnificent coral color, delicate layered arabesques or stylized vines, 9' x 13'. Estimated value $16,000.

Iran, vegetal dyes, 10' x 14'. Estimated value $19,000.

Iranian village rug, vegetal and chrome dyes. Wool warp and weft, prayer design, 6' x 9'. Estimated value $6,200.

Iran, vegetal dyes. Old Persian vase design with lotus leaves or palmettes, 9' x 13'. Estimated value $16,000.

Iran, vegetal dyes. Unique tribal or village rug with charming little animals and trees, 9' x 12'. Estimated value $9,500.

Turkey

While there is a paucity of rug weaving in Turkey that may be the result of increasing gentrification, this country is still producing some very interesting rugs today. Vegetal dying, which radically changed the new rug industry in 1983, began in Turkey. Important vegetal-dyed carpets with hand-spun wool are now being woven throughout Turkey. Also, fine vegetal-dyed Turkish kilims are available that are among the best in the world.

Turkey, close-up, vegetal dyes. Glorious, vital colors, excellent wool.

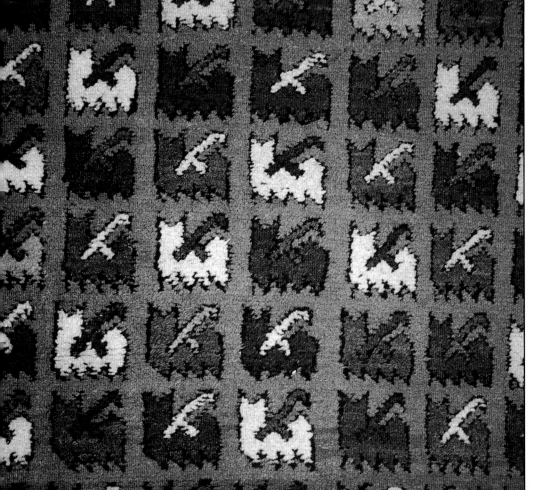

Turkey, close-up, vegetal dyes. Cheerful colors, localized village pedigree.

Some of the most important new rugs from Turkey are the vegetal-dyed old northwest Persian Heriz, Serape, and Mahal reproductions, perfectly and exactly executed. Some of these natural-dyed carpets with hand-spun yarn have soft, pale hues and others have more saturated colors. Since they are exact reproductions in every respect of what are some of the most important antique rugs extant, and because they have discernible workshop pedigree, they may very well be collectible carpets of the future. Because they have a short pile and low knot density, they are a little delicate and thus are not sufficiently appreciated by the American public.

Some of the best fine new vegetal-dyed rugs in old Caucasian designs are also being made in Turkey today. Synthetic chrome dyed village rugs, the staple of rugs from Turkey, are also quite excellent, but perhaps not quite as interesting as the vegetal-dyed products.

Turkey, close-up, vegetal dyes. Probably old northwest Persian rug design.

Turkey, close-up, vegetal dyes. Old northwest Persian rug design.

Turkey, vegetal dyes. Western influence fosters Eastern individual rather than group expressiveness, 5' x 8'. Estimated value $3,200.

Turkey, vegetal dyes. Wool warp and weft. Lively colors, localized village pedigree, 6.8' x 6.8'. Estimated value $3,200.

Turkey, vegetal dyes. Design derived from old northwest Persian Tabriz rug, 6' x 9'. Estimated value $4,000.

Turkey, vegetal dyes. Classical rust, blue, and ivory colors. Close reproduction of old northwest Persian Serape rug, 9' x 12'. Estimated value $8,800.

Turkey, vegetal dyes. Thick overlapping thin spiraling arabesques. English Arts and Crafts design, 9' x 13'. Estimated value $8,500.

Turkey, vegetal and chrome dyes. Balanced abrash or color changes. Good spacing between designs, 8' x 11'. Estimated value $4,000.

Turkey, vegetal dyes. Center medallion, open field design. Dramatic abrash or
color variation. Cloud band border, 8' x 10'. Estimated value $3,600.

Turkey, probably chrome dyes, 6' x 9'. Estimated value $2,500.

Nepal & Tibet

There has been a great deal of interest today in modern designed rugs from Nepal. Nepalese rugs are now the most rapidly growing group of hand-made Oriental carpets in the world.

These contemporary, abstract designed carpets are primarily a color rather than design art. While the designs may be quite unique, these carpets represent the purist form of color art in carpets to-day. Since designs are simple or sometimes not even present, color is the key to understanding these carpets.

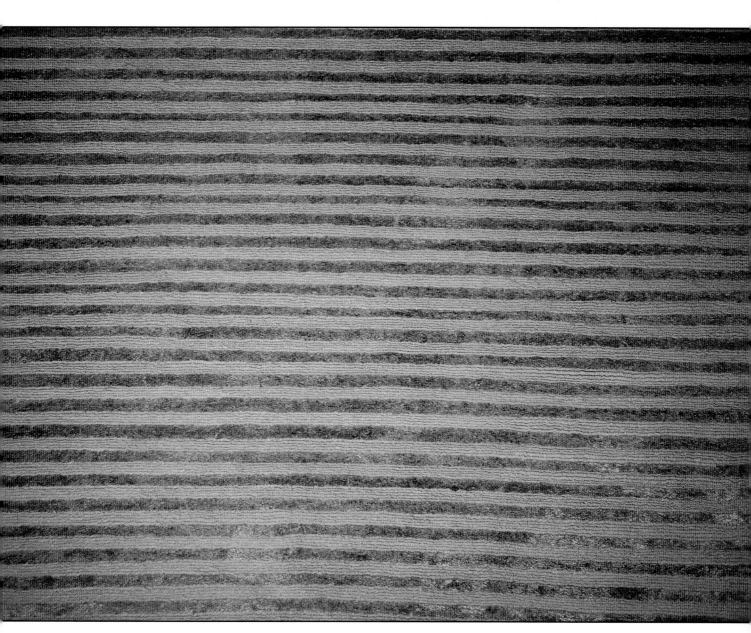

Nepal, close-up, chrome dyes. Mixed weave with silk pile and wool wrapped wefts.

Buyers should try to find examples with the most exquisite colors and unique shadings. Subtle color changes within or between colors and inlaid silk add uniqueness and personality to the rugs.

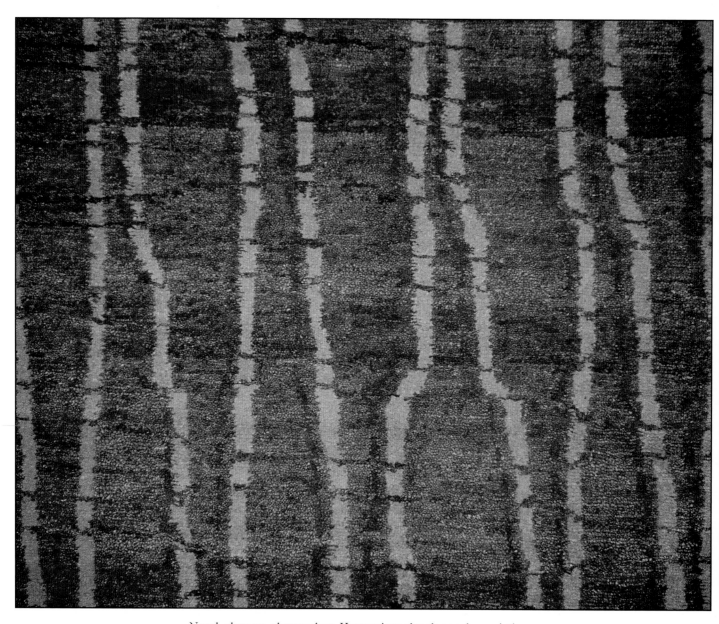

Nepal, close-up, chrome dyes. Harmonious abrash or color variations.

Opposite page:
Top: Nepal, close-up, chrome dyes. Wool and silk.

Bottom: Nepal, close-up, chrome dyes. Wool and silk.

The wool from Nepalese mountain sheep is probably the second best in the world and is soft and lanolin rich. Only New Zealand may be superior to Nepalese wool. The "handle" or touch of these rugs is very soft and this is an important reason for their popularity today. Some Nepalese rugs have a good deal of silk but the wool in the best carpets is about as soft as the silk. The foundation warp and weft threads tend to be fairly thin but are elastic and quite well twisted. They are capable of great stability and durability over time, particularly if padding and a vacuum cleaner that is not too powerful are employed.

The great advantage of Nepalese carpets is that the simplicity of the designs may obviate the necessity for an interior designer as these rugs are generally easier to color coordinate than traditional rugs from India, Pakistan, Iran, or China. These rugs may also appeal to many people who want a change or object to the "Granny" look of traditional carpets owned by their parents or grandparents. Since they often have simple repeat patterns without borders they may be placed under, adjacent, or away from the sofa without fear of creating an imbalance in the room. Ironically, while Nepalese rugs are quite commercialized, they appear to be unique, unusual, and expressive, and these qualities also account for their great appeal today.

Nepal, close-up, chrome dyes.

Colors with a complex cast or wool that is over-dyed for added depth may be exceptionally beautiful and collectible if the designs are also especially elegant and beautiful. Unfortunately, the more complex and beautiful the cast of the carpet color, the more difficult the color match. Unusual colors are difficult to identify and names must often be made to describe them such as reddish coral, greenish ivory, or brownish taupe. When coupled with good design structure, the resulting carpet may be quite stunning. More neutral colored Nepalese rugs may be quite beautiful but not as striking as the more uniquely colored carpets. Nepalese rugs are made with lab produced synthetic chrome dyes in which potassium dichromate is the mordant that fuses the dyes to the wool.

Nepal, close-up, chrome dyes. Self tone with thin alternating rows of wool and silk.

Tibetan carpets are similar to Nepalese, but are decorated in traditional Tibetan designs. While Nepalese rugs are generally made with chrome dyes, Tibetan rugs are vegetal-dyed. Unlike Nepalese rugs, which are quite plentiful, there are not many Tibetan carpets being woven today. Tibetan rugs are generally quite beautiful and are stylistically similar to the magnificent old Chinese Peking, Ningshia, and Ming rugs, which, unfortunately, are not reproduced at the present time. Small sized Tibetan rugs may be particularly lively, cheerful, and dynamic with important old symbols from Tibet and China that are perfectly reproduced.

Nepal, close-up, chrome dyes. Traditional Tibetan lotus design.

Nepal, chrome dyes. Wool and silk, 6' x 9'. Estimated value $2,500.

Nepal, chrome dyes, 6' x 9'. Estimated value $1,200.

Nepal, chrome dyes, 6' x 9'. Estimated value $1,700.

Nepal, chrome dyes, 6' x 9'. Estimated value $2,000.

Nepal, chrome dyes, 9' x 12'. Estimated value $3,700.

Nepal, chrome dyes. Wool and silk, 9' x 12'. Estimated value $6,000.

Nepal, chrome dyes, 6' x 9'. Estimated value $2,500.

Nepal, chrome dyes. Mixed weave with wool pile and wool wrapped wefts, 9' x 12'. Estimated value $6,000.

Nepal, chrome dyes. Good, balanced abrash or color variations, 9' x 12'. Estimated value $6,000.

Nepal, chrome dyes. Wool and silk, 9' x 12'. Estimated value $5,000.

Nepal, chrome dyes. Lotus or palmette design, 9' x 12'. Estimated value $6,000.

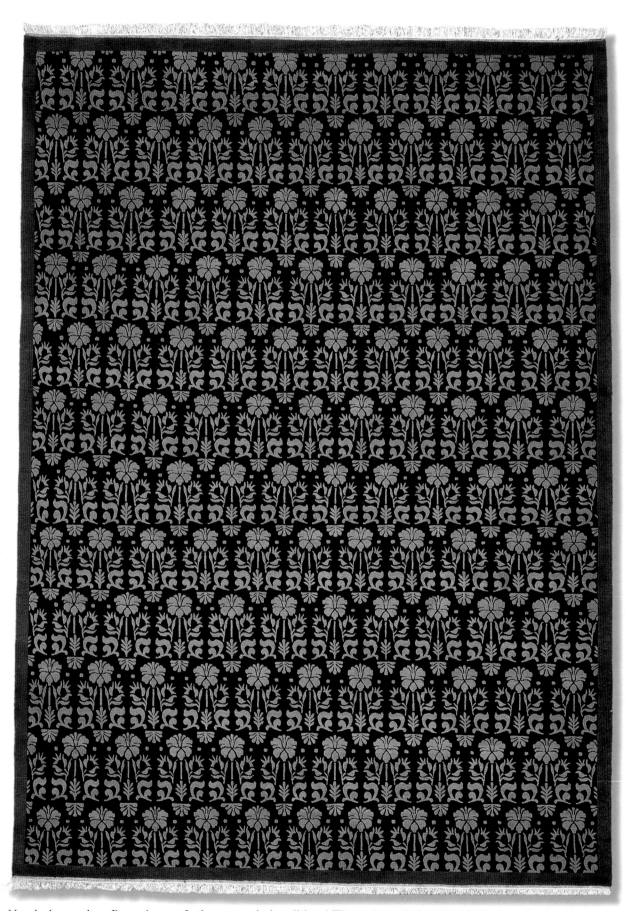

Nepal, chrome dyes. Repeating, perfectly symmetrical traditional Tibetan lotus design, 9' x 12'. Estimated value $5,000.

Nepal, chrome dyes. Silk pile, warp, and weft. Traditional Tibetan lotus design, 8' x 11'. Estimated value $10,000.

Nepal, vegetal dyes. Traditional Tibetan design. Lotus flower in center, bats in corners, 3' x 5'. Estimated value $1,000.

Nepal, vegetal dyes. Traditional Tibetan or Chinese designs, 3' x 6' each. Estimated value $1,200 each.

Tibet, vegetal dyes. Traditional Tibetan or Chinese symbols, 6' x 9'. Estimated value $3,200.

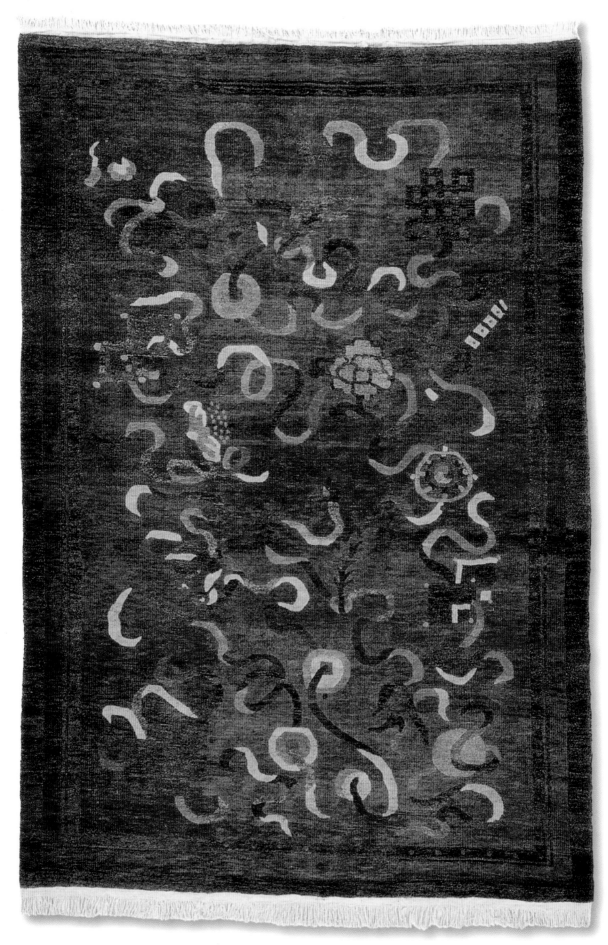

Tibet, vegetal dyes. Cloud band design, 6' x 9'. Estimated value $3,200.

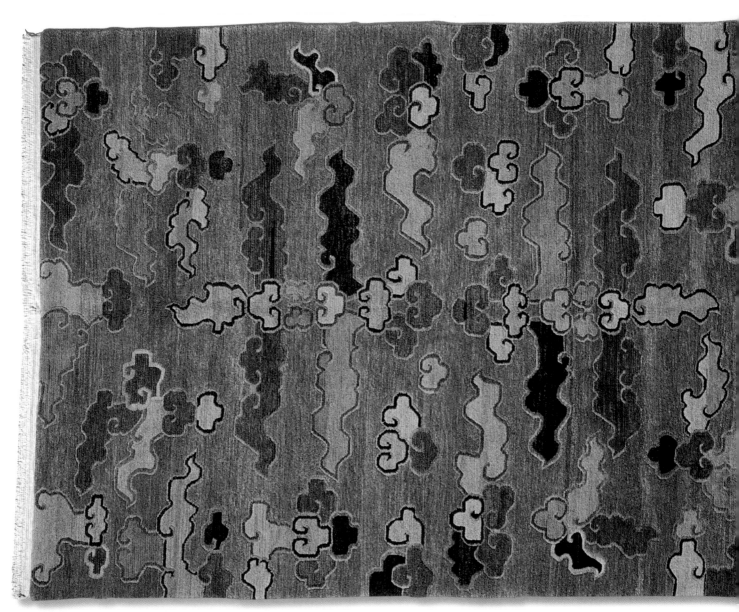

Tibet, vegetal dyes. Cloud band design, 6'
x 9'. Estimated value $3,200.

Tibet, vegetal dyes. Traditional Tibetan floral motifs. Economy of colors, 6' x 9'. Estimated value $3,200.

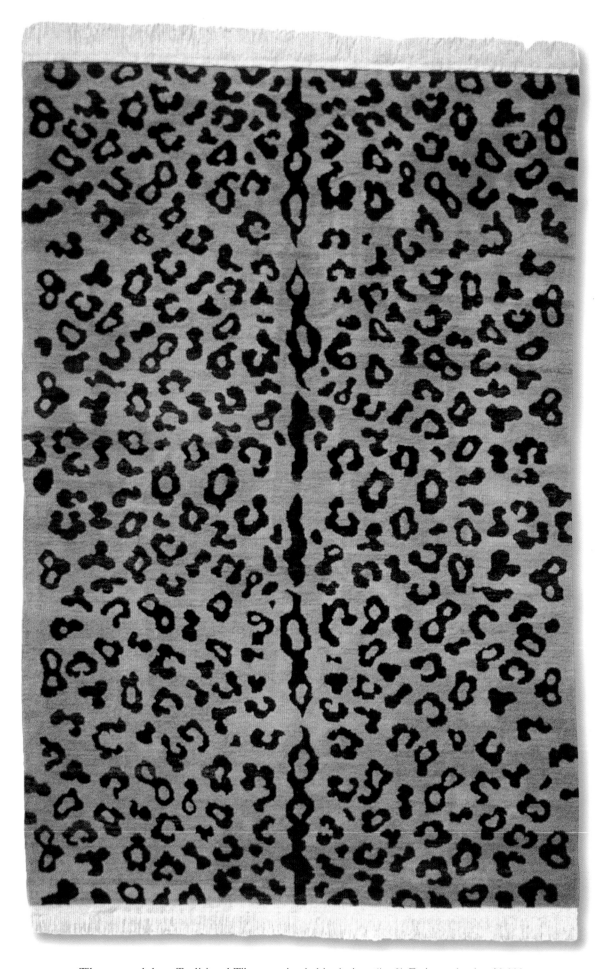

Tibet, vegetal dyes. Traditional Tibetan animal skin design, 6' x 9'. Estimated value $3,200.

Tibet, vegetal dyes. Traditional Tibetan stripe design, 9' x 12'. Estimated value $6,000.

Tibet, vegetal dyes.
Traditional Tibetan
designs, 6' x 9'.
Estimated value $3,200.

Tibet, vegetal dyes.
Wool and silk.
Stylized traditional
Tibetan and modern
floral motifs, 6' x 9'.
Estimated value
$4,000.

China

China arguably produces some of the best lower priced floral rugs at about $35 a square foot or approximately $3800 for a 9 x 12 foot carpet at retail. They have clean and crisp designs and a light wash to retain sharp, well-defined outlines around the motifs. They are generally faithful reproductions of great old Persian rugs and the innovations, when added, are usually quite successful.

Silk is inlaid around the edges of the flowers to add definition. They work well with all types of furniture; however, the colors may be a little too fresh for distressed leather sofas.

These very popular carpets are solid floor coverings for growing families and may last fifty years or more with padding, vacuuming, rotation, and periodic commercial cleaning about every five years. The wool is well washed and the quality control is the best in the industry.

Abrash, or color change within individual hues, is absent, and all colors are perfectly uniform. Uniform colors were desired in Persian city carpet prototypes from Tabriz and Kashan throughout the twentieth century. Abrash has only become popular in recent years, primarily in new village carpets.

China, close-up, chrome dyes. Silk highlights.

Finer Chinese wool and silk carpets contain more silk and are also good values at higher price points. Some of these rugs may have flowers entirely in silk and are good investments that are very similar to Persian city carpets of proven value that are made with wool and silk. The best new Chinese wool and silk rugs with high silk content have a slightly lighter weight, but are otherwise almost indistinguishable from similar fine Persian Tabriz carpets.

Lamentably, almost no new Chinese wool carpets in old traditional Chinese designs are being made today. New producers of carpets in China do not appreciate the importance of old Chinese Peking carpets in the old rug trade. Therefore they are not reproducing these magnificent carpets with simple understated elegance and a lot of open space surrounding a few large motifs.

Thick, heavy, and plush, Chinese hand-carved rugs have gone down in price in recent years. These very popular rugs are quite durable if good quality examples are purchased at about $25 a square foot at retail. They should not be bought in the least expensive, lowest grade with dry, finely spun yarns as they tend to lose too much pile and color with successive commercial washings over time.

Similarly new Chinese carpets in old French Savonnerie designs are among the best and closest replicas woven today. Even many medium grade Chinese reproductions of antique Savonneries compare favorably with the very expensive prototypes from Europe. Low grade Chinese Savonneries, like inexpensive Chinese hand-carved rugs, may also lose too much wool and color when commercially washed and should be avoided.

China is beginning to produce new antique-washed rugs and kilims in geometric designs and will probably develop more fine antique-washed floral carpets in the near future.

China, close-up of center medallion, chrome dyes. Silk warp and weft. Fine weave, silk flowers and highlights.

China, chrome dye
Fine weave with si[lk]
warp, weft, and
flowers, 6' x 9'.
Estimated value
$6,800.

China, chrome dyes. Old French
Savonnerie design, 6' x 9'. Estimated value
$2,500.

China, chrome dyes. Old French
Savonnerie design, 6' x 9'. Estimated
value $2,000.

China vegetal dyes. Soft patina and understated elegance, 9' x 12'. Estimated value $6,000.

China, vegetal dyes. Exquisite color, complex, delicate overlapping arabesques or stylized vines, 10' x 14'. Estimated value $9,000.

China, vegetal dyes. Innovative designs and colors, 10' x 11'. Estimated value $6,300.

China, vegetal dyes. Unusual and decorative main field color, 9' x 12'. Estimated value $6,800.

China, vegetal dyes. Distinctive and well drafted, 9' x 13'. Estimated value $7,500.

China, vegetal dyes. Harmonious with good abrash or color variation, 9' x 12'. Estimated value $6,800.

China, vegetal dyes. Lotus or palmette design, soft, beautiful colors, 10' x 13'. Estimated value $8,000.

China, vegetal dyes. Alluring, with successful color and design innovations, 9' x 12'. Estimated value $6,800.

China, vegetal dyes. Old Persian tree-of-life court design. Cheerful colors, 10' x 14'. Estimated value $9,000.

China, vegetal dyes. Lively and cheerful colors, 8' x 10'. Estimated value $5,000.

Many good carpets are made in Egypt and Rumania today. Although some may have lively and cheerful colors, Egyptian carpets are usually the palest rugs woven in the industry. They are generally reproductions of rare and important antique Persian Mahal, Indian Agra, and Turkish Oushak carpets. They have a medium weave and a short pile or nap. Their strength lies in the fact that they are distinguishable, unique, and quite consistent rugs with magnificent and unbelievably soft colors. The weakness is that the wool in some Egyptian carpets tends to be a little dry and thus slightly less durable than the wool found in many other rugs. Carpet padding and rotation is recommended if an Egyptian, or any other rug, is purchased for the home.

Egypt, close-up, probably chrome dyes. Soft, pastel colors.

Egypt, close-up, vegetal dyes. Special wash to achieve extra-soft patina. Lotus or palmette design.

Rumanian rugs also have the advantage of being distinctive and inimitable. Some have cheerful colors and are made with vegetal dyes and wool rather than cotton foundation threads. These rugs may utilize soft, lanolin rich wool that is imported from Turkey. Others are chrome dyed and made with domestic Rumanian wool. They have extremely well drafted and executed designs that are uniform and rigorously symmetrical. Rumanian wool is slightly better than Egyptian, but is still rather dry when compared with wool from other parts of the Near and Far East. Better wool will be employed in all major workshops in Rumania in the very near future.

Rumania, close-up, vegetal dyes. Turkish wool pile, warp, and weft.

Rumania, close-up, chrome dyes. Crisp design.

177

Egypt, vegetal dyes. Lotus or palmette design. Undulating serrated leaf border motifs, 9' x 12'. Estimated value $9,500.

Egypt, vegetal dyes. Old northwest Persian rug design, 10' x 14'. Estimated value $12,000.

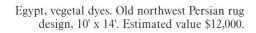

Rumania, chrome dyes. Well drafted and spaced motifs, 8' x 10'. Estimated value $6,000.

Rumania, chrome dyes. Elegant and highly symmetrical, 9' x 12'. Estimated value $7,800.

Rumania, chrome dyes. Refined and proportional European floral designs, 6' x 9'. Estimated value $4,000.

Chapter Three
Minor Rug Types

Kilims or Flatweaves

New kilims or flatweaves are not appreciated as much as they should be in the United States today. This is perhaps because they appear to be delicate, consisting of warps and wefts only without pile knots in between. But just because they feel thin does not mean they are fragile, short-lived investments. In fact, dollar for dollar, the better examples are among the best values in Oriental rugs today. Fine vegetal-dyed Persian soumak kilims, with areas of embroidered pile, sold for about $60 a square foot, are some of the best carpets in the market. A soumak kilim, which consists of colored wefts wrapped around rows of warps, is woven in a more complex manner than the simple kilim.

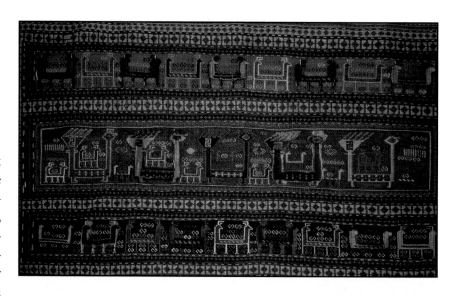

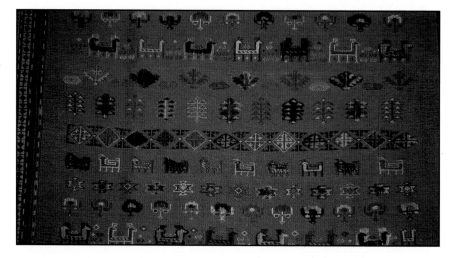

Top to bottom:
Iranian soumak flatweave, close-up, vegetal dyes. Embroidered pile. Fine and highly detailed.

Iranian soumak flatweave, close-up, vegetal dyes. Embroidered pile. Charming small animal and plant motifs.

Iranian soumak flatweave, close-up, vegetal dyes. Close reproduction of rare old Caucasian soumak.

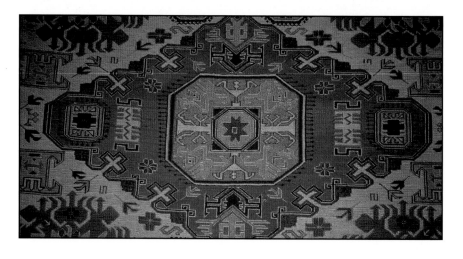

Great success has also been achieved in new Chinese kilims and soumak kilims in a wide range of different grades. While they may not have the collectible value of the Persian soumaks, they are fine values at the lower price points.

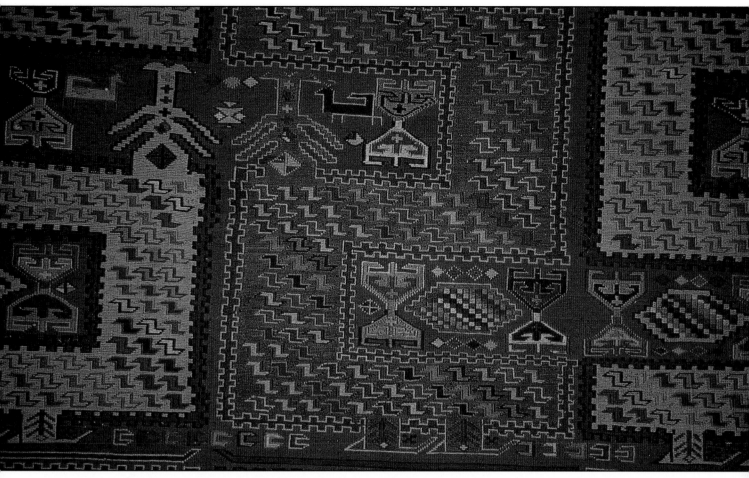

Chinese soumak flatweave, close-up, chrome dyes. Stylized dragon design. Close reproduction of rare old Caucasian soumak.

Chinese flatweave, close-up, chrome dyes. Symmetrical design and economy of color.

There is a lot of variation in the quality of new kilims, but designs are generally surprisingly well rendered. The following are some advantages of investing in kilims for the home: they condense fine quality in portable, densely packed, interlocking warp and weft threads, have a thin old rug sensibility, employ archaic rectilinear abstract designs from highly coveted old rugs and kilims, and are ideal in casual settings. The success of the design sets and the flow of colors are easy to sense or analyze, and the quality of many of the better examples is self-evident to the neophyte rug connoisseur.

Turkish flatweave, close-up, vegetal dyes. All wool. Deep, saturated, cheerful colors. Fine weave.

Unlike pile carpets whose colors often change with the direction of incoming light, kilims look the same when viewed from the ends or sides. This reduces decorating problems that arise from the direction in which the pile carpet is placed.

Turkish flatweave, close-up, vegetal dyes.
All wool with wool embroidery. Old
Bessarabian kilim design.

Turkish flatweave, close-up, vegetal dyes.
All wool, old Bessarabian kilim design.

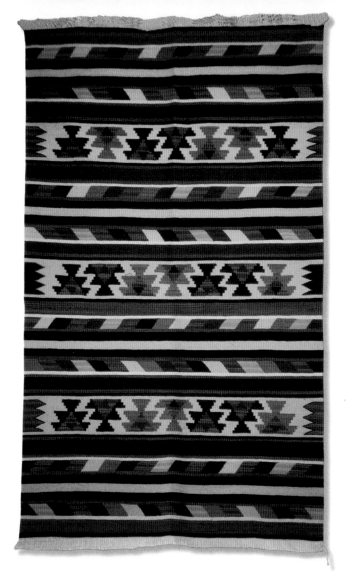

Chinese flatweave, chrome dyes. Old Caucasian design, 3' x 5'. Estimated value $150.

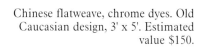

Chinese flatweave, chrome dyes. Old Caucasian design, 3' x 5'. Estimated value $150.

Chinese flatweave, chrome dyes. Old Caucasian design, 3' x 5'. Estimated value $150.

Chinese soumak flatweave, chrome dyes. Fine weave, delicate draftsmanship and harmonious colors, 6' x 9'. Estimated value $2,000.

Chinese soumak flatweave, chrome dyes. Interesting design innovation and decorative colors. Good spacing between motifs, 6' x 9'. Estimated value $1,700.

Rumanian flatweave. Vegetal and chrome dyes. All wool, highly stylized lotus or palmette design, 8' x 10'. Estimated value $2,700.

Indian soumak flatweave. Chrome dyes, jute warp and weft. Fine weave, pure and vivacious colors, 6' x 9'. Estimated value $1,200.

Needlepoint & Aubusson

Good quality new Chinese needlepoint and Aubusson flatweaves are excellent values today. Many are very close reproductions of rare, important, and valuable antique English needlepoint and French Aubusson flatweaves. The prices are also lower than they were a few years ago because large retailers are buying directly from China. Aubussons are more expensive than needlepoints but more durable and difficult to weave so the price difference is justified; however, needlepoints generally have great internal contrast and vitality, and work particularly well with country English or French decor.

Chinese needlepoint flatweave, close-up, chrome dyes. Lively colors, three-dimensional flowers.

Chinese Aubusson flatweave, close-up, chrome dyes. Soft patina.

The quality of needlepoint and Aubusson flatweaves is more difficult to evaluate and this explains their relatively high rate of return in retail stores. Many Americans do not appreciate the beauty and value of these flatweaves because they have never seen the originals.

Chinese needlepoint flatweave, close-up, chrome dyes. English Arts and Crafts design.

Chinese Aubusson flatweave, close-up, chrome dyes. Powerful center medallion.

Although both types are quite durable, particularly when purchased with a padding, they do appear to be too thin and delicate when viewed by the novice rug buyer. In order to allay the client's anxiety about these fine flatweaves, they must be properly presented to the client.

Chinese needlepoint flatweave, close-up, chrome dyes. Compartment and garland design.

Chinese Aubusson flatweave, close-up, chrome dyes. Center medallion.

There is great variation in the quality of needlepoint and Aubusson flatweaves as some are much better than others. Buyers should try to see what the old examples look like in order to properly analyze the reproductions. A good salesperson is important in order to find beautiful and elegant needlepoint and Aubusson flatweaves with soft, yet robust colors and designs that follow closely upon priceless early English and French prototypes.

Chinese needlepoint flatweave, close-up, chrome dyes. Lively three-dimensional flowers.

Chinese Aubusson flatweave, close-up, chrome dyes. Powerful and colorful.

Needlepoint and Aubusson flatweaves may be very pale but should still be alive and not look too flat or boring. Although there are many excellent pale needlepoint and Aubusson flatweaves in the market, generally crisper designs with higher definition and contrast are safer investments. Since many of the old examples are so beautiful, the perfect reproduction is rarely run-of-the-mill.

Unfortunately, strange and unsuccessful design and color innovations are sometimes found which are particularly harmful to the flow and overall elegance of these weavings. Good new needlepoint and Aubusson flatweaves have good detail, with an elegant and classical rather than regimented and mechanical appearance.

Chinese needlepoint flatweave, close-up, chrome dyes. Aubusson design.

Opposite page:
Top: Chinese needlepoint flatweave, close-up, chrome dyes. African floral design. Pale and attractive.

Bottom: Chinese Aubusson flatweave, close-up, chrome dyes. Good definition and detail.

Chinese Aubusson flatweave, chrome dyes. Harmonious design with good local interest, 6' x 9'. Estimated value $2,000.

New Chinese wall tapestries which are reproductions of complete old Belgian, French, and Flemish tapestries may be excellent investments today. They are not appreciated by the American public but are not really very expensive at all. The better ones have great detail and very closely approximate the originals.

The quality of the reproductions may vary but many can be found which have perfectly drawn faces, animals, and trees. One bad design may be problematical, but if it is not disturbing, and the rest of the designs are realistic and perfectly rendered, the tapestry may still be quite acceptable. If two or more designs are not well drawn and drafted, or look odd, an otherwise excellent tapestry may fail. If animals or people look oversimplified, overly ordered, or out-of-scale, the tapestry has been inadequately reproduced. Trees and leaves are usually quite well rendered in reproduction French or Flemish verdure tapestries.

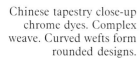

Chinese tapestry close-up chrome dyes. Complex weave. Curved wefts form rounded designs.

Chinese tapestry, close-up, chrome dyes. Realistic and well drafted.

Like needlepoint and Aubusson flatweaves, tapestries should have life, good colors, and contrast lest they also appear dull and lifeless, without the continuous local interest and stimulation found in the great old tapestries of the past.

Chinese tapestry, close-up, chrome dyes. Good detail, life-like subject, well rendered.

Opposite page:
Top: Indian silk, close-up, chrome dyes. Compartment, prayer, and tree-of-life designs.

Bottom: Indian silk, close-up, chrome dyes. Silk warp and weft. Hunting scene design, layered arabesques or stylized vines.

Silk Rugs

Silk rugs are generally more expensive and slightly less durable than wool rugs. They are also more difficult to repair when they are old and worn; however, silk rugs are, in the long run, usually better investments than wool rugs for those who can afford them. They can be very finely woven with exceptional detail and very high definition. They are as close as one can get to the great old rugs of the past that were woven for the shahs and sultans in the early court ateliers. Silk is always a plus in carpets and, in general, high silk rugs are better and more expensive than medium or low silk rugs, which have a lower silk content.

Silk rugs, historically, were rare, expensive, and highly collectible because it was difficult to procure silk for carpets. Because it is easier to produce silk fiber today, silk rugs, while expensive, are actually quite cheap if the old carpet market is the yardstick for evaluating them.

In the old rug trade occasionally only small silk rugs from the late nineteenth and early twentieth centuries are found. Now it is amazing, from the old rug dealer's perspective, to see so many room-sized silk rugs on the market today.

India, China, Pakistan, Iran, and Egypt produce beautiful floral silk rugs that should be considered by buyers who can afford rugs at higher price points. Some very interesting silk rugs with geometric designs are also being produced in India. The special sheen and glow of colors shimmering in the light changes so dramatically to a darker tone when the silk rug is viewed against the pile from the dark side.

Indian silk, close-up, chrome dyes. Silk warp and weft, unusual geometric design silk rug.

Indian silk, close-up, chrome dyes. Silk warp and weft. Garden, compartment, and tree-of-life designs.

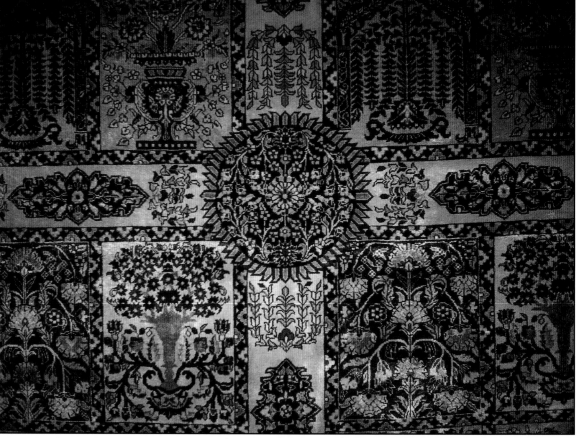

Look for silk rugs with the most crisp and sharply defined patterns, preferably in old classical designs with little to no questionable innovations. The most educated buyers today generally appreciate the self-evident quality of floral silk carpets and are correct to believe that the best examples, if well bought, are safe investments.

Chinese silk, close-up, chrome dyes. Silk warp and weft. Center medallion, over 350 knots per square inch.

Chinese silk, chrome dyes. Silk warp and weft. Very fine weave, glowing and lustrous pile, 4' x 6'. Estimated value $2,500.

Chinese silk, chrome dyes. Silk warp and weft. Very fine weave, high definition. Small, delicate flowers, 3' x 5'. Estimated value $1,500.

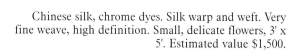

Chinese silk, chrome dyes. Silk warp and weft. Very fine weave, unusual smooth,
extra soft texture. Interesting design innovation, 6' x 9'. Estimated value $4,000.

Machine Made Rugs

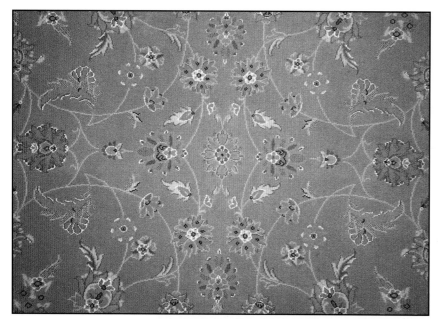

Just as new handmade rugs in their beauty are getting closer and closer to the great antique rugs of the past, new machine made rugs are beginning to look more and more like new handmade rugs. The design definition is improving every year and the mechanistic appearance of ornamentation is being reduced.

Belgian machine made close-up, chrome dyes. Elegant and refined.

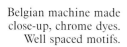

Belgian machine made close-up, chrome dyes. Well spaced motifs.

Belgian machine made, close-up, chrome dyes. Classical paisley or boteh design.

The abrash, or color change within individual hues, used to be garish and mechanical, but is now getting more subtle and graduated. The feeling of machine made rugs is now more organic or rustic and a soft antique patina is successfully being rendered.

Producers of new handmade rugs are a little jittery over the improvements in machine made rugs as they pose a significant threat to the sale of hand knotted rugs. Machine made rugs are now the staple of many Oriental rug retailers.

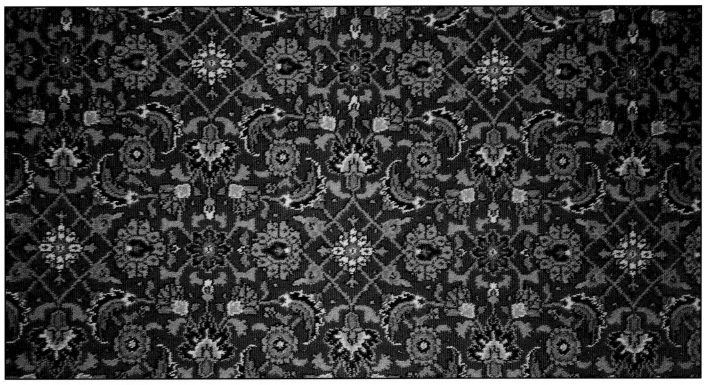

Belgian machine made, close-up, chrome dyes. Classical herati design. Life-like and similar to handmade rugs.

Belgian machine made, close-up, chrome dyes. Antique patina. Analogous to soft, decorative, handmade rugs.

Some extremely fine machine made rugs with either wool or synthetic pile are exquisite, have very sharp designs, and superb color and design harmony. They are indeed a difficult challenge for the handmade rug industry today. They may be very durable with hard backs and heavily bodied, densely packed wool.

Machine made rugs do not have the problems of consistency or quality control that are found in handmade rugs. The strengths of machine made carpets are the traditional strengths of handmade carpets, namely durability and consistency or quality control.

While machine made can never achieve the subtlety of design and color found in many of the better handmade carpets, the introduction of vegetal-dyed wool to the machine rug industry in the not-too-distant future will be an exciting and challenging development.

Belgian machine made, close-up of center medallion, chrome dyes. High wool density, excellent quality. Hundreds of thousands of points, or tufts of fibers per square meter.

Belgian machine made, close-up, chrome dyes. Closely resembles many fine handmade floral rugs.

Belgian machine made, chrome dyes, 5' 7" x 7' 10". Estimated value $1,000.

Belgian machine made, chrome dyes. Lotus or palmette and serrated leaf designs. 5' 7" x 7' 10". Estimated value $1,000.

Belgian machine made, chrome dyes. Jute warp and weft. One million points or tufts of fibers per square meter. 5' 7" x 7' 10". Estimated value $800.

Belgian machine made, chrome dyes. Jute warp and weft. 5' 7" x 7' 10". Estimated value $800.

Belgian machine made, chrome dyes. Jute warp and weft. Lotus or palmette, cloud band, and arabesque or stylized vine designs. 5' 7" x 7' 10". Estimated value $800.

Belgian machine made, chrome dyes. Unusual design, 5' 7" x 7' 10". Estimated value $900.

Hand tufted rugs are improving every year and becoming an increasingly significant and important part of the Oriental carpet market. If the hand and machine made rug industry is viewed in its totality, hand tufted rugs are the fastest growing group of Oriental carpets today. The artistry of these rugs is in the individual designer or creator because the simple and pure method of weaving does not require a great deal of skill. Yet the future may ultimately be in the simplicity and purity of hand tufted carpets. They can be manufactured anywhere in the world and artists can create paintings underfoot in modern abstract designs in an unlimited manner.

Yarns are tufted with a small hand or large electric tufting gun. The gun has a large needle that pushes and pulls threads of wool through a heavy canvas back upon which a design has been drawn. Indian hand tufted rugs are made slowly and almost entirely by hand with a small hand gun. Chinese hand tufted carpets are made more quickly with a large compressor machine. Indian tufted rugs thus have a more personal touch than their Chinese counterparts.

Tufted rugs are similar to hand hooked and needlepoint rugs in which the design is painted on a mesh foundation before weaving. Whereas in hooked rugs the wool surface loops are not sheared, in tufted rugs the loops are sheared off and the resulting rug has the appearance of a thick pile carpet. Latex is used to adhere the wool to the canvas, and the back of the rug is generally covered with heavy cotton to hide the rough and unsightly foundation. The cotton backing is the signature of the hand tufted carpet.

Some of the best hand tufted rugs are very popular and contain high quality wool and silk. They may rival many handmade carpets in beauty and quality. Many hand and machine made rug producers are trying to perfect hand tufted carpets in the quest to create the best 9 x 12 foot rug that retails for $2000. This sometimes leads to a difficult choice for the rug buyer in that it may be hard to decide between a high grade tufted or low grade handmade carpet.

The great advantage of the hand tufted carpet is in its thickness and low price. The disadvantage is that some have more durable and long-lasting latex backings than others. It is advisable to buy good quality tufted rugs as the latex is better and will not dry out over many commercial cleanings. While tufted rugs are strong, they are generally slightly less durable than machine made carpets in which the pile is more solidly fused into the foundation. Since pile fibers may be pulled out of hand tufted rugs, they cannot be recommended over machine made carpets for people with pets. The best quality hand tufted rugs may last up to fifty years of heavy use if properly maintained.

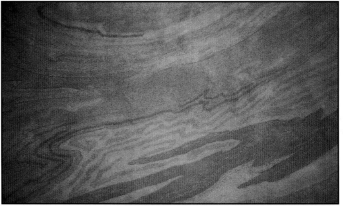

Chinese hand tuft, close-up, chrome dyes. Contemporary abstract design.

Chinese hand tuft, close-up, chrome dyes. Unlimited creativity.

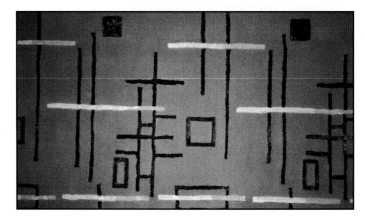

Chinese hand tuft, close-up, chrome dyes. Contemporary abstract design.

Indian hand tuft, chrome dyes, 6' x 9'.
Estimated value $600.

Chinese hand tuft, chrome dyes. Wool
and viscose, 6' x 9'. Estimated value
$1,000.

Chinese hand tuft, chrome dyes. 70% wool and 30% mercerized cotton, 6' x 9'. Estimated value $1,000.

Indian hand tuft, chrome dyes. Lotus or palmette and serrated leaf designs, 6' x 9'. Estimated value $800.

Chapter Four

Rug Buying

Home Trial

Home trial is now given by most major Oriental carpet retailers. A rug may usually be tried at home for one week and returned for a full refund if it does not work successfully. More than one rug may be tried at the same time for the same space if one cannot decide in the showroom which carpet works best with the fabric.

Many clients have fabric problems that only home trial can solve. The more beautiful the colors in the rug the more likely that the slight color shadings will not be accurately rendered in the showroom. A rug that is greenish-blue in the showroom may be bluish-green at home. Home trial allows for viewing the rug from many angles and lighting circumstances in the morning, afternoon, and night. A pale rug may look better in a room with less sunlight and a more colorful rug may be preferred in a room with more sunlight.

One may find that the rug chosen may be used in a different room. By living with the rug for a week one may find that one can tolerate color and size problems that at first were intolerable. A rug that touched the inlaid trim of the hardwood floor on the sides but not on the ends may be accepted by the end of the trial week. A rug that seems a little too

large or small but is loved by the clients may also be eventually accepted. Similarly, the preferred carpet might also be tolerated, with time, even if the cast of the carpet colors does not blend perfectly with the color shadings found in the sofa. In this sense, home trial is the moment of truth for the carpet selected.

Nepal, close-up, chrome dyes. Elegant and refined design.

India, close-up of center medallion,
chrome dyes.

215

The ability to match colors is no substitute for understanding carpet quality and one should, if possible, never sacrifice quality for complementarity with adjacent fabrication. For the past 100 years the American housewife has attempted to blend a carpet to other carpets or fabrics in the home. Because houses in the United States tend to be large, the plentiful adjacent fabrics to the rug have assumed a greater importance than in Europe where homes tend to be smaller. The more beautiful the rug, the more tolerant the color coordinator should be with the adjacent fabric.

The problem is that carpet quality has often been sacrificed because superior rugs may not blend as well as more prosaic rugs. Because wall treatments predominate in the United States, pale rather than lively colors and low rather than high design definition has achieved a greater importance, sometimes to the detriment of greater carpet quality. If more lively rugs are selected, with more detail and definition, they may more likely become valued antiques in the future and valued testimonials to the taste of the owners.

Since the carpet may become a valued antique, consumers should ideally begin with the rug. Unfortunately, this creates logistical problems in the sense that the adjacent fabric that is special ordered after the carpet may not be of the right color cast. Thus, for convenience, consumers usually start with the furniture and paint chips and end with the rug that is portable and easily returned to the retail store.

Consumers in the United States are more interested in the art of matching fabrics than they are in the art of the carpet. The logic of their position may be justified by the amazing fact that most Oriental carpets have great durability. Very coarse India carpets with about forty knots per square inch or less, that should retail for no more than $25 a square foot, may remain in good condition in the home after forty years of hard use without a padding. An entire family might grow up with such a carpet. The medium grade Indo-Jaipur from India with about fifty knots per square inch, which sells for about $35 a square foot at retail, could conceivably last much longer.

Since the American buyer does not for the most part have to worry about durability, and since he is not really interested in buying for investment, he or she is free to concentrate entirely upon color coordination with adjacent fabrics. This is where the American consumer proves his or her mettle.

The best customer for the salesman is the compliant or loose coordinator. Such a person is sensitive but can quite readily tolerate a degree of disharmony when he or, more likely, she attempts to match the fabric to the carpet. She may return a carpet to the store from which it was purchased if someone tells her it does not work but she herself has no problem with a match that is not very close. A banana colored leather sofa with gold highlighted pillows may be quite acceptable to such a person. Kelly green pillows with fairly similar green in the carpet is also acceptable to this kind of buyer. Only the general value of the colors need to harmonize with one another but the tones within the colors matched do not have to perfectly coordinate.

The compliant coordinator may not even like rugs that harmonize too closely with fabric, finding such a home environment an excessively formal affectation. Her home is usually warm and lived in with framed pictures in abundance and all manner of ornament all over the place. This buyer, because of her flexibility, is poised to buy a good quality rug that may have better long-term investment possibilities than the critical color coordinator with the more limited selection of possible carpets at her disposal.

The compliant coordinator should not be confused with the person who knows nothing about matching the fabric to the carpet and is completely lost. This is the confused color coordinator. This may be a difficult customer who needs proof as to which fabric works and why and is not easily convinced because of a lack of sufficient sensitivity. Her best hope is to find a furniture expert whom she can trust to lead her to the right fabric.

Many men are also confused coordinators who could not color decorate a room, no less a house, without an interior decorator. While confused at first, some men may be easily convinced if they can sense that the room appointments do not fight one another.

Most carpet buyers are critical color coordinators. This buyer is not tolerant of discordant color and may return several rugs after trying them at home. The housewife that is a critical color coordinator will not simply accept a color in the carpet that is a cousin of a very similar color in the fabric. Whereas the compliant coordinator will accept a color in a rug that is a distant relative of the color in the fabric, the critical coordinator will only accept a color in a rug that is a fraternal twin of the color in the fabric.

This housewife will not accept a fabric color which is merely a darker or lighter version of the color in the carpet. She expects the cast of the color in the fabric to be very similar to that of the carpet. She knows when the fabrics fight one another and expects very little fighting between them. She has an unpleasant feeling when colors do not blend very closely in all lighting situations and may also be concerned about texture matching.

The critical coordinator often has a sixth sense about matching the rug to the fabric. This intuition allows this client to perfectly and almost effortlessly match colors. While red or brownish wood furniture and a leather sofa can sometimes create significant coordinating problems, the critical coordinator can usually sense if the rug works in the environment. She also can sense if the rug is too light or too dark for the sofa or floor. The critical coordinator correctly varies rugs from room to room but coordinates them stylistically: Formal floral with other formal or stylized floral (rectilinear floral) rugs, and geometric with other geometric or stylized floral rugs but not with formal floral rugs.

The felt sense of harmony varies from person to person depending upon individual tolerances. Conflicts may occur between husbands and wives as they debate whether color clashes are present.

If an ivory colored Tibetan carpet is tinged with green, the critical coordinator senses that it fights with certain leather sofas but may work with a neutral black sofa. A beautiful, uniquely colored rug may compel the critical coordinator to open up other more limited but excellent and challenging possibilities for adjacent fabrication.

The compulsive color coordinator is a person who is never satisfied with the match between the rug and the fabric. This person may spend years looking for that perfect match, which unfortunately only exists in the mind but not in reality. The cast of a particular color of the carpet must exactly match the cast of the fabric. Whatever tones are found in the solid field color of the carpet must be picked up in the fabric. Blue is often the color that compulsive coordinators cannot tolerate as well as any other colors or designs that stand out even slightly against the background. A rug that is only slightly lighter than the chair fabric may be rejected for that reason. A rug may be perceived as too wide, narrow, large, or small when it actually works quite well in the space.

The compulsive coordinator believes that if the red color of the carpet contains a hint paprika and a dash of tomato those colors must also be found in the fabric when the rug and fabric are viewed from all directions in all lighting circumstances. The texture of both room appointments must also be identical which is impossible since the pile of the carpet has a luster that is different from the flat woven fabric. This inner-directed carpet client is unflappable and unaffected by appeals to common sense. This client is not influenced by the salesperson's appeal that "Life is too short" or "It's only a carpet" and will not give up the impossible mission.

The compulsive coordinator's anxiety may also be manifested when rugs are rejected for a little dirt, a tiny speck or two, for having fringes, and for having fringes that are too light or longer at one end than the other.

To make matters worse, some compulsive color coordinators feel that they must try to perfectly match the carpet not only to existing fabrics but to other fabrics that may be added at a later date. Since they do not know what fabrics may be purchased in the future they often give up the chase at this point and buy neutral beige or gray wall-to-wall carpeting.

India, close-up, chrome dyes. Lotus or palmette design.

Nepal, close-up, chrome dyes. Simplicity and purity of popular self-tone rug.

Indian hand loom, chrome dyes. Hand crafted with shuttle loom. Shag rug, 6' x 9'. Estimated value $700.

Small is Sensible

There has been a growing interest in new smaller rugs in the last few years. Very large rooms may have two or more living areas each with distinctly different rugs that are related to one another by design and color. A twenty by thirty foot room may employ two 8 x 10 or 9 x 12 foot carpets rather than one oversized rug. This allows for greater creativity, variety, and flexibility within large rooms.

Proportionately more smaller rugs for larger rooms are being sold today than 12 x 15 or 12 x 18 foot carpets. Since many people are buying and selling homes or furnishing more than one home, the 8 x 10 or 9 x 12 foot carpet is safer and more practical than the more limiting 12 x 18 foot carpet.

If the homeowner is certain that he does not plan to buy a larger home at a later date, he may choose the oversized carpet, which may be an excellent value. Since oversized carpets have higher list prices, greater discounts may be available for 12 x 15 or 12 x 18 foot rugs. Some retailers may discount large and expensive carpets more severely if sufficient profit can be made on them.

Scatter rugs, around 4 x 6 feet are also more popular today. If the buyer has a budget of about $1500 to $2000, a superb 4 x 6 foot rug may be purchased from any of a number of different countries. It is best not to scrimp on the purchase of a small rug as a considerably better piece may often be bought for just a little more money.

Iran, vegetal dyes. Wool warp and weft. Local pedigree from town of Bidjar, 4' x 7'. Estimated value $4,000.

Comparison Shopping

Comparison shopping is a good idea only if the price of the same rug is being compared. Even so, one rug from a particular workshop may have better wool or wash than another rug of the same sort from the same workshop. One rug may have a higher knot count than another with the same design, or one rug with a lower knot count may have a better wash and thus be more desirable than the same rug with a higher knot count.

When comparing two different rugs from two stores, try to find the best quality rug for the space by comparing the contents of the main field, main border, and guard borders for elegance, precision, and beauty. This is a difficult decision because one may prefer the main field color of one rug and the main border design of the other. Or one may prefer the design of the guard borders of one rug, but the main border of the other.

Since the first impression of the carpet is so important, the buyer must also try to sense which rug has the greatest emotional appeal. A strong positive initial reaction augers well for the long-term feedback or benefit that the rug will provide.

Iran, close-up, vegetal dyes.

Nepal, close-up, chrome dyes. Mixed weave with wool and silk pile and wool wrapped wefts.

Good Salesperson

Since quality is difficult to determine with surety and since comparison shopping is consequently often ineffectual, the knowledgeable, trustworthy salesperson, within a reputable store, assumes great importance in the purchase of a carpet. The good salesperson should be able to answer questions and justify the price he asks for the carpet without hesitation. His job is not simply to match fabric but to find the best quality rug to match the fabric. The honest salesperson adds value to the rug and knowledge of and belief in the carpet selected by the client with truth rather than deception.

The good salesperson knows what the original old carpet, which inspired the new reproduction, looked like. He can thus determine if the reproduction is faithful to the coveted antique prototype. If innovations have been made in the reproduction, the good salesperson will be able to determine if the innovations were successful and explain that to the client. He or she will be able to explain to the client, if asked, which of the two or three final rugs selected is more successful and why.

The knowledgeable salesperson will always respect the client's taste but might urge him or her to never forsake a great rug that is a little too small or large for the room. The experienced salesperson will also know why a modern sofa might look better adjacent to or slightly over a rug while a classical legged sofa might work well half or entirely on top of the carpet. Or, the salesperson might assist in understanding why a shiny textured fabric might be more suitable with a lustrous silky wool carpet.

In some situations, the reliable salesperson might obviate the need for an interior designer. This may be advantageous, for while many interior designers are valuable and competent time savers for busy over-achievers, some may be a little too pushy. When they present their viewpoints, interior designers should not rob the client of his or her own perspective. They may suggest many possible options, but should leave the final decisions to the client so that the client may put his or her personal imprimatur on the project.

Since many salespersons do not have sufficient knowledge of antique rugs, rug buyers should study old rug books, if possible, to get a sense of why certain antique rugs are sold and resold at high prices, in various states of repair, in the old carpet market and in auctions today.

India, close-up, vegetal dyes. Old Persian Bidjar design.

Pakistan, close-up, vegetal dyes. Economy of design and color.

Chapter Five

Rug Care

Rug Wear

Wear is the greatest concern of old rug dealers when they purchase antique carpets. Generally, old rug traders will not buy worn carpets unless they are very old, rare, and important.

It is thus particularly important for the novice rug buyer, if possible, to prevent wear from occurring in the new carpet purchased. The general rule is the lower grade or more commercial the carpet, the more essential that it remains in perfect pile. The better the carpet, the more forgiving a future dealer may be about a slight lowering of the pile in a few areas of the rug.

Because of increased commercialization of most new rugs woven today, no wear to the foundation may be tolerated by future rug traders. With very few exceptions, only the new rug that remains in perfect condition has a chance of retaining value in the future.

The proof of the need to take very good care of new rugs is derived from the analysis of commercial rugs that are bought and sold in the old carpet trade. Seventy-year-old machine made American Wilton carpets, if they are traded at all, are only bought and sold by dealers if they are in perfect pile. Good quality sixty-year-old commercial grade Indian carpets with repeating boteh or small paisley designs are also traded only when they survive in full pile. Similarly, seventy-year-old medium grade Turkish Sparta carpets, in old Persian Sarouk designs, are also traded only when the nap is unblemished. Even old higher commercial grade carpets, such as seventy-year-old Persian Sarouks and milles fleurs Kermans, Art Deco or Nichols Chinese and other categories of good old rugs, had to remain in perfect condition to be of any real interest to the old rug trade.

Fine new rugs with very short naps, or rugs that are sheared to the foundation in areas to replicate the sense of an antique carpet, may also be collectible if they are particularly distinctive and beautiful.

Rugs must be rotated 180 degrees occasionally to prevent the slight and almost imperceptible lowering of the pile in certain areas of high traffic. If a rug looks much better from one direction it may face that way for a longer period of time than the less pleasing direction. Padding will allow one to keep a rug in the preferred direction longer provided that areas are not being over-exposed to very heavy traffic or excessive sunlight. All rugs should still be turned around at least a few times in the course of their very long life spans.

Many antique-washed rugs will get a little darker as fibers are brushed off the light surface through walking, vacuuming, and commercial cleaning. This is probably good since the dark generally looks slightly better than the light side.

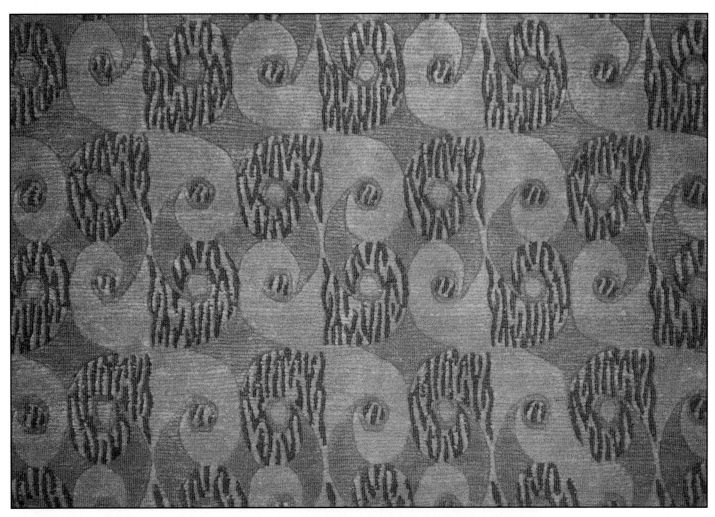

Nepal, close-up, chrome
dyes. Unusual design,
harmonious colors.

India, close-up, chrome dyes.
Pile sheared very low to
reproduce texture of old rug.

Rug Cleaning

Stains should be blotted immediately with a clean dry sponge or paper towel and then blotted again with club soda or seltzer water on a clean sponge or cloth. Then the excess water should be blotted yet again with a sponge or paper towel.

Old stains may be removed with Capture dry carpet cleaner or Afta which is also known as Oops. Afta may be rubbed up and down and from side to side into the fibers quite briskly but never rub too much even if the stain remains as the fibers may be damaged.

Dilute Oxiclean may only be used on synthetic chrome but not vegetal-dyed carpets. Oxiclean will read the vegetal dye as a carpet stain and color may be removed from the wool. It is a good idea to spot test a small area before applying all stain removers.

Silk rug stains should be blotted immediately with a sponge or paper towel and gently wiped with a clean, slightly water dampened sponge or cloth. Then brush Capture into the stain, allow to dry for a few hours, and vacuum the Capture out of the rug.

Unlike wool, silk must remain as dry as possible throughout the stain removing process. Capture may also be used on old stains in silk rugs. If one has any doubts about how to clean a particular stain one should immediately contact a reputable carpet cleaning facility.

Rugs must be commercially cleaned every three to five years to prevent moth damage and clean out partially embedded stains and dirt that were not completely removed before. Commercial cleaning may be delayed for over five years if the owner is meticulous about removing stains as soon as they occur. The commercial cleaning process is quite vigorous and apt to slightly loosen the structure of the carpet, reduce color intensity, and dry out the fibers, making them more susceptible to wear; therefore, it is best to delay this procedure as long as possible while not subjecting the rug to the dangers of moth damage or color loss from residual embedded stains.

The true test of the quality of the carpet is in the commercial cleaning and one of the best arguments for buying a better quality rug is that it washes well.

Chinese soumak flatweave, close-up, chrome dyes. Center medallion, old Caucasian design.

Nepal, close-up, chrome dyes. Compartment and stylized tree-of-life designs.